CW01497413

Praise for

RELATIONSHIP CURRENCY

"In today's world, we are craving human connection. This book is the answer. Once you learn the five communication habits Ravi masterfully lays out, it won't just change your career or business—it will change your life."

> **GERARD ADAMS,** cofounder of Elite Daily and CEO of Leaders Create Leaders

"*Relationship Currency* is essential for anyone who wants to build stronger, more genuine relationships with prospects, customers, or their team. Ravi is a natural storyteller and true professional who breaks down the art of communication with clarity and passion. His approach makes complex concepts feel simple and practical, with his personal stories bringing each habit to life. If you want to elevate your sales game and connect with people on a deeper level, this book is an absolute must-read!"

> **MICHELLE FAISON OLDHAM,** national sales director, T-Mobile

"Ravi is a master at turning relationship-building into an actionable skill that anyone can learn. *Relationship Currency* shows his unique ability to blend clarity, care, and integrity into communication frameworks that build lasting trust. If you want to elevate every conversation and connect on a deeper level, this book is for you."

> **BEN MEER,** founder of System Sunday

"Having hired Ravi to deliver a keynote speech at our Sales Kickoff, I can say this book proves he truly practices what he preaches! *Relationship Currency* offers a fresh, compelling, and insightful take on building business relationships with integrity. A must-read for anyone looking to master the art of communication."

> **LISA BONO,** team lead, global sales productivity, Oracle NetSuite

"In a world increasingly shaped by AI, the demand for genuine human connection has never been greater. But how do you build trust, ask better questions, or tell stories that truly resonate? Ravi's masterful book doesn't just teach these skills; it transforms how you approach every business relationship."

> **SAMANTHA MCKENNA,** CEO of #samsales Consulting

"*Relationship Currency* is a master class in how to communicate for connection, build trust, and create authentic business relationships. Ravi offers a fun, tactical, and people-centric way to help you connect with others in a meaningful way. This is a must-read!"

JEN ALLEN-KNUTH, sales keynote speaker and founder of DemandJen

"Ravi should be working with your company just like he did with ours! He not only brings magnetic charisma and lives what he teaches, but during his keynote, he captivated a multicultural audience of hundreds. Afterward, we applied his storytelling framework from Habit 4 and immediately saw a difference in how our teams connect with prospects and customers. If you want to communicate with impact, spark intentional conversations, and build meaningful business relationships, read *Relationship Currency*. You'll thank me later!"

ROBERTO BONORA, regional senior business director, Sherwin-Williams

"Influence isn't about tricks, it's about trust. *Relationship Currency* gives you a road map for building the kind of trust that drives real change. It's wise, actionable, and actually fun to read! Meant for all of us who want to connect deeper and have meaningful conversations."

DR. ZOE CHANCE, bestselling author of *Influence Is Your Superpower*

RELATIONSHIP CURRENCY

RELATIONSHIP CURRENCY

FIVE COMMUNICATION HABITS
FOR LIMITLESS INFLUENCE
AND BUSINESS SUCCESS

RAVI RAJANI

amplify
an imprint of Amplify Publishing Group

www.amplifypublishinggroup.com

Relationship Currency: Five Communication Habits for Limitless Influence and Business Success

The author has tried to recreate events, locales, and conversations from their memories of them. In order to maintain their anonymity in some instances, the author has changed the names of individuals and places, and may have changed some identifying characteristics and details such as physical properties, occupations, and places of residence.

For more information, please contact:
Amplify Publishing, an imprint of Amplify Publishing Group
620 Herndon Parkway, Suite 220
Herndon, VA 20170
info@amplifypublishing.com

ISBN-13: 979-8-89138-966-3

Printed in United States

Dedicated to my daughter and son.

Thank you for inspiring me to be a better man.

This is for you.

CONTENTS

MASTER AND EMBODY WHAT'S IN THIS BOOK

"Do you want to join the all-boys dance class, Rav?" my mum asked. My heart was thumping, and my inner people-pleaser was cowering, yet my nine-year-old self obediently smiled and nodded. (Have you ever tried saying no to an Indian mum who doesn't take no for an answer? Didn't think so!)

Anthony, the owner of my little sister's dance school, had a vision of starting an all-boys dance class and needed five recruits to make it a reality. His infectious energy, pearly white smile, and flamboyant demeanor inspired action, leaving my mum with no choice but to fulfill his desire. The only loser in this arrangement was me (or so I thought).

Looking back, those dance classes were pretty damn fun! Was I going to be Britney Spears's next backup dancer? Hell no. Did I feel like I was living a "double life" at school with my dirty little secret? Hell yes. But I can't deny it—I had fallen in love with the stage. But after twelve short months, a James Bond–themed showcase and my secret being exposed to everybody in school (a story for another day), I quit.

Here's what else is true. Whether she knew it or not, my mum had Miyagi'd me. If you're a *Karate Kid* fan, you know exactly what I'm talking about. "Wax on, wax off." Unknowingly, I had been learning a skill that would later serve me for life: the art of stage presence.

Flash forward several years, and my childhood friend's father (a playwright by night) wrote me into his first play. Ram knew I'd never had formal acting lessons or experience, nor did he care. From a few lines here and there, to lead roles and the opportunity to perform at the National Youth Theatre in London, once again, I had been Miyagi'd. Whether he intended to or not, Ram was the one who first exposed me to the art of public speaking and story-telling, a set of skills that would once again serve me for life.

Thinking back and connecting the dots, I realize that every single experience was happening *for* me, not *to* me. Every trusted guide was secretly preparing me for the next chapter of my story, compounding the very skill that would later become my edge: the art of communication. But here's the unwanted truth: it all began decades ago.

Mastery of any new skill requires you to embark on a lifelong journey and delay gratification in a world obsessed with overnight success.

As you begin to embody the five communication habits so you can build trust, earn relationship currency, and unlock more of what you desire, the question is this: Are you willing to play the long game?

THIS IS A MARATHON, NOT A SPRINT

Most books walk most readers through a section on "how to use this book." But this isn't most books, and you're not most readers.

I don't want you to "use" this book. Instead, I'm inviting you to implement the practices laid out in this book and commit to a lifestyle of mastery. Just like my mum, Ram, and all of the trusted guides in between who Miyagi'd me, I'm about to repay the favor, my friend. As you consume each habit with intentionality, you'll begin learning and compounding new communication skills that will serve you in the next chapter of your story. To truly get the most out of this experience, you'll need to trust the process; decondition yourself from what you believe about influence, communication, and relationship building, and fall in love with the imperfect journey that lies ahead. Remember: Anything achieved overnight can leave you overnight. The beauty lies in delaying gratification and doing the work.

Oh, and by the way, if reading this book serves a vanity metric that you've self-imposed (such as consuming fifty-two books in fifty-two weeks), let's hug it out and part ways. That trophy isn't on offer here. If you're still reading, then I invite you to begin your journey with purpose. If at any point you find yourself drifting away, lacking presence, and itching for hacks, gimmicks, or tricks, close the book and live to fight another day. Revisit the learnings tomorrow. I will not cast any judgement, my friend.

MOVING FORWARD WITH AN OPEN MIND

What you'll notice along the way is that the journey to tapping into your limitless influence is secretly a personal development expedition in disguise. You'll be met with resistance, the reality of your internal narrative, and new frameworks for thinking, which may clash with your current view of the world. Welcome it; that's where growth lies. If you approach this process with an open mind, you just may question a belief or story you've been telling yourself that has been subconsciously sabotaging your personal and professional success. As you review your deepest convictions, be open to questioning their validity and how they may be limiting your choices, decisions, and mindset in a way that's preventing you from receiving more of what you say you desire.

On the other side of this experience lies another version of you who's able to ethically, organically, and masterfully earn relationship currency by communicating with influence, so you can receive more prosperity in your career or business.

At the end of the day—or the end of this book—both of our perspectives and views of the world can coexist in harmony. My intention isn't to give you a one-size-fits-all method that lacks context, personalization, and nuance. Instead, I'm offering you "my truth" rather than attempting to enforce my thesis as a "universal truth." My North Star is to empower you to use this book as a compass to find "your truth," so you can embody the five habits without disowning your energy, swagger, or true voice.

As you engage in the deep work necessary for personal growth and communicating with influence, you're going to have to learn, implement, and iterate the practices laid out in this book. This will require you to adopt a new set of behaviors. At a fundamental level, the consistent repetition of these behaviors is what will form new habits. However, as you'll soon learn, change can be messy. As they say, we are the problem, and the solution. When you take ownership of your journey and fully embrace the habits proposed, not only will you create true change, but you'll achieve both personal and professional transformation. In a nutshell, as your level of competence increases as an influential communicator, the world will become your oyster. In light of that, I invite you to measure your growth alongside the conscious competence learning model.

HOW TO MEASURE YOUR GROWTH: CONSCIOUS COMPETENCE LEARNING MODEL[1]

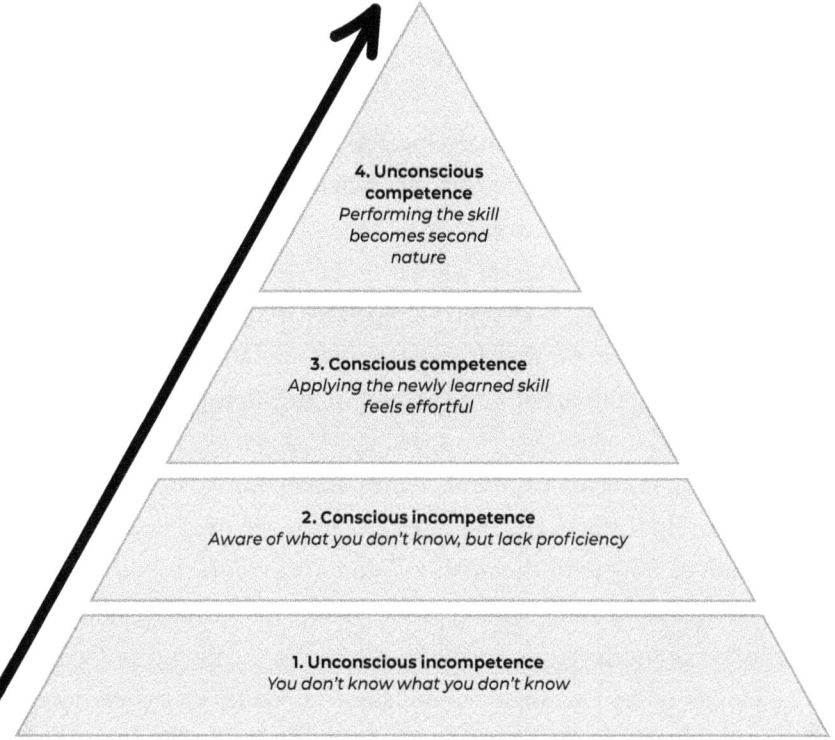

4. Unconscious competence
Performing the skill becomes second nature

3. Conscious competence
Applying the newly learned skill feels effortful

2. Conscious incompetence
Aware of what you don't know, but lack proficiency

1. Unconscious incompetence
You don't know what you don't know

CONSCIOUS COMPETENCE LEARNING MODEL

Some of you may be familiar with the Conscious Competence Learning Model (CCLM). For those who aren't, let's get acquainted.[2] The CCLM's origin is widely disputed; however, it's largely attributed to Noel Burch in the 1970s. It illustrates the stages someone moves through when learning a new skill. The first stage of this model is at the bottom of the pyramid (learning a new skill) and moves to the top of the pyramid (mastering the skill that was once new).

The first stage, Unconscious Incompetence (ignorance), is about learning a new skill for the first time. At this stage, you don't know what you don't know and may even reject the usefulness of this new skill. I see it as uncovering hidden blind spots that are crushing your ability to achieve your desires.

The second stage, Conscious Incompetence (awareness), is where you are actively aware of your incompetence and are willing to engage in trial and error to gain more awareness. Through imperfect action and real-life mistakes, you learn and tweak for success.

At the third stage, Conscious Competence (learning), you have the tool kit to apply this new skill. Implementation may feel robotic, clunky, and awkward at times, but we all know that growth isn't linear. Sometimes we need to slow down to speed up. At this stage, this new skill will still require conscious effort and mental firepower to execute.

At the final stage, Unconscious Competence (mastery), you're in a state of flow with the new skill and are able to embody it on autopilot. But this isn't the end point. This is the starting point for a lifestyle of mastery.

Here's what I've seen among the thousands of people I've trained, coached, and mentored. At a conceptual level, they acknowledge and identify that mastery is a journey, not a destination. However, when it comes to integrating the new behaviors required to form the communication habits proposed, they secretly expect overnight results. When they don't achieve unconscious competence almost instantly, they convince themselves that the cost of change outweighs the cost of staying exactly where they are. Shortly after, they revert to the status quo, as that's where comfort lies. This causes them to spin their wheels; they continue to do more of what doesn't work, achieving the same results they've always gotten. Consequentially, their level of competence remains stagnant, their growth stalls, and internal chaos ensues.

What I'm saying is this: Change is difficult. Not changing is difficult. Choose your difficult. I'm giving you all I've got inside these pages—mainly the knowledge and know-how—but you're the one who must go out there and slay, my friend. Remember, knowledge isn't power; knowledge that is implemented and iterated is power.

As you take imperfect action, market feedback will support you in tweaking your approach to align with your authentic self. Before you know it, you'll have achieved unconscious competence in the very thing you once struggled with and will be effortlessly communicating with influence and using it as a gateway for earning relationship currency: the key to everything you desire.

WHERE ARE MY PEOPLE AT?

Now, who are you—the person on the other side of these pages, reading these very words? You may identify with the traditional labels of entrepreneur, leader, salesperson, or customer service professional. However, as you'll soon learn, I'm not a huge fan of titles or labels.

I care about your essence as a human being. You're impact-driven and purpose-oriented. You care about building meaningful business relationships that last a lifetime. Yes, you're a go-getter, but you want to operate with integrity and in a way that doesn't violate your values. You want to increase your influence in an ethical way.

Let me repeat that: *in an ethical way.*

You're sick of surface-level interactions, transactional behavior, and conversations rooted in hidden agendas and lacking connection.

You want to embody a people-centric approach to earning relationship currency by communicating for trust. You're conscious. You're intentional. And you're committed to a life of internal growth. Ultimately, you know that to achieve your version of prosperity, your primary job is to help others achieve more of what they desire, allowing abundance to organically find you in return.

Have I got you figured out? Excellent. Then you're in the right place. I am happy you're here, and I know we are going to get along just great. Welcome to the movement.

YOU ARE IN
THE PEOPLE BUSINESS

*"We're in the people business serving coffee, not the coffee
business serving people."*

—HOWARD BEHAR, *retired president of Starbucks*

When used with integrity, communicating with influence
helps you build trust. Trust helps you *earn* relationship
currency (notice how I didn't say "win"?). And relationship
currency is the key to getting more of what you desire in business (and in life). That's it—mic drop. This is the premise this
entire book stands on.

Let's break it down, shall we?

You've probably picked up this book because you believe
communicating for trust will help you achieve more of what
you desire. The question is what do you want in this season of
your life? Nope, not what your friends, family, or society want
for you. I'm asking you—what do you truly want for your
career or business?

Maybe it's receiving a promotion, being perceived as a
transformational leader, or driving business growth at your

company. To protect these external outcomes from being driven by scarcity, approval-seeking, or an unhealthy ego, I invite you to find solitude, calm your nervous system, and give yourself permission to dream big as you ask yourself what you truly want.

I'm talking about embodying that childlike energy where you can tap into your limitless imagination without conditioning from the outside world. To avoid analysis paralysis and self-judgment, move toward whatever feels exciting, energizing, and expansive in this chapter of your story. As you evolve, so will your desires, and that's okay.

Plot twist. Your desire may arrive through an unexpected path (and that's a good thing). When you remove your death grip on how things "should" look, you stop chasing, surrender control, and open yourself up to receiving what's truly *meant* for you. Paradoxical? Yes, but let's go deeper.

Want to land a leadership role at your company? As you pursue this desire by climbing the corporate ladder, you may realize that being an individual contributor is where your true genius lies. As you welcome this unexpected path, internal joy finds you, and you become a thought leader in your field.

Want more revenue growth? As you pursue this desire by trying to acquire new customers, your hypothesis is proven incorrect, and you stumble upon an explosive growth opportunity from deepening relationships with existing customers. As you welcome this unexpected path, revenue growth finds you, and you build a profitable business for the long term.

What I'm trying to say is this—be fixed on the desire, but flexible on the path. As you identify your desire and build momentum toward a path you think will energize you in this chapter of your story, I invite you to remain open to life's signals, which may point you toward an unforeseen road to achieving said desire (or pivoting altogether—desires may change over time as you grow).

Rigidly holding on to how you want things to look sucks (been there, done that, and received the trophy). If you're trying to build trust with others, it begins with trusting yourself first. With me?

For clarity, for the remainder of this book, I'll refer to your external goals as "desires" and the ways in which you could receive them as "paths." Oh, and by the way, if you'd like to gut check if your desire is driven by an unhealthy ego state or not, ask yourself this simple question: Is my desire rooted in instant gratification? More on this shortly.

So, how do we achieve said desire through an aligned path? By building meaningful relationships that matter. If you're an entrepreneur who wants to raise money, there's another human being you're going to have to connect with who's going to write you a check. If you're a salesperson who wants to sell a product or service, there's another human being that holds the purse strings. And if you're a leader who wants to rally people around a common vision, you need to collectively connect with a group of human beings and inspire them to take action.

Remember this: Another human being holds the keys to your kingdom; they are what unlock the doors to your desire(s). Yes, that's right, my friend—human beings. Not AI, growth hacks, or secret playbooks.

RELATIONSHIP CURRENCY:
THE ONLY CURRENCY THAT MATTERS

"We're in the people business serving coffee, not the coffee business serving people."[3] These thirteen words were once uttered by Howard Behar, the former president of Starbucks, indicating a powerful mindset: being people-centric is a way of life. Take a moment to try it on for size. You're in the people business doing what?

As you embody this mantra, you'll instantly humanize your conversations, meetings, pitches, and presentations. The result? Uncovering a deep knowing that authentic relationships are everything in business (and life). Authentic relationships include two human beings willingly building and strengthening the connective tissue required to form a meaningful bond, without experiencing an *imbalanced energy exchange*. These final three words are everything.

Think about it like this: while somebody holds the keys to your kingdom, you also have the keys to theirs. Meaning, building meaningful relationships is not a one-way street. Embodying this concept is key for understanding what relationship currency actually is. Relationships are sacred. Currency carries connotations of transaction. However, side by side, relationship currency is about engaging in a meaningful value exchange that helps somebody achieve more of what they desire, without self-interest, allowing the energy of abundance to organically find you in return. In its purest form, you don't buy or acquire relationship currency; you earn it. This is how you unlock true prosperity. Here's a million-dollar case in point.

Aaron Krause, the founder of Scrub Daddy, is the genius behind those smiley-faced sponges you see in your local supermarket. In the early-ish days, Krause knew he was on to something but was unable to get his product into retail stores, because he was missing one key ingredient: the "who." He had the "how" down due to his inventor's mind, entrepreneurial flare, and manufacturing experience; however, no matter how amazing his product or expertise was, he needed another human being—the "who"—to help him meet his desires.[4] Enter the TV show *Shark Tank*.

"I know exactly what I need to do to make this thing really efficient, and I'm looking for a strategic partner who can open this up to the retail stores . . . I'm only in five supermarkets, that's it!" This was part of Krause's nail-biting pitch back in 2012. Not only did he unapologetically own his genius, but he was clear on his major blind spot. He knew he needed the right Shark, with the right relationships, to explode his business.

Here's where things got spicy. As a bidding war ensued, Daymond John made an offer contingent on Lori Greiner's involvement in the deal. Why? Because John knew this product was in Greiner's area of excellence, and she had the strategic relationships to take it all the way. Greiner could smell John wanting to ride her coattails and profit off of her hard-earned relationship currency, which led her to dismiss him in a flash.

In Greiner's own words to Krause, ". . . Connections are everything." In the end, Krause accepted Greiner's proposal of $200,000 for 20 percent equity.[5] To date, Scrub Daddy has been one of the most successful companies to appear on *Shark Tank*. According to *Fortune, On Demand*, Scrub Daddy achieved north of $220 million in sales for 2023, and Krause stated that he was just getting started.[6] And what about Greiner? It's estimated that the "Queen of QVC" has earned a 250–300 times return on her investment, with her original 20 percent stake now being worth an estimated $50 to $60 million.[7]

Here's why this story matters to our conversation.

I once heard, "It's not the how that matters, it's the who." Krause seemed to understand that the "how" would be trivial if he could unlock the "who," also known as the meaningful relationship required to unlock his desires.

And if you look closer, Krause's example proves this energy exchange was far from imbalanced. Krause landed a strategic relationship to open himself up to retail stores and expand his vision, while Greiner added a diamond in the rough to her portfolio, which was the gateway to accelerated wealth creation. Remember, if somebody has the keys to your kingdom, you just might hold the keys to theirs. This entire story is a potent illustration of the power of relationship currency.

Here's what most don't know: Krause's smiley sponge was initially rejected by a Fortune 500 company, and his invention gathered dust *for years* until *Shark Tank* entered the picture.[8] This is a perfect example of pursuing a desire without being attached to a singular path to get there. Scrub Daddy's story wasn't one of overnight success, but one of delayed gratification.

Along Krause's journey of going from pain to glory and becoming the hero of his own story, he had to overcome a series of hurdles, obstacles, and setbacks. As you embark on the journey that lies ahead, I invite you to welcome the challenges that are inevitably coming your way. Why? They are a necessary requirement for creating the friction needed to initiate a transformation. Without them, we cannot expand our being and become the type of person that's able to receive and sustain our desires. Every story requires both a hero and a villain. The villain in our story isn't a human being. It's instant gratification. The question is, who will be victorious?

THE VILLAIN IN OUR STORY: INSTANT GRATIFICATION

Behind every TV show, movie, play or book you love is an intentional story arc (something we'll discuss in Habit 4). As any compelling narrative unfolds, a clearly identifiable hero and villain emerge. The villain's job is to inflict pain and create conflict, to agitate the hero, and prevent them from achieving their version of success. If the villain had it their way, the hero would follow a path of misalignment, live in a state of internal chaos, and never achieve the transformation they deserve.

The villain in our story—mine, yours—isn't a person, it's society's obsession with instant gratification. I'm talking about our addiction to chasing overnight success and receiving our desires "now." Explosive sales growth? We want it now. A role in the C-suite? We want it now. Mastery of a new skill? We want it now (you know that itch you're experiencing to skip straight to the first communication habit? Say hello to instant gratification).

We can binge-watch an entire season of a new show on Netflix in a weekend; we can order restaurant-ready food to our door in less than twenty minutes; and we can become an overnight sensation on social media if we make the algorithm our friend. If most things are just a click away, why can't the same be said for our deepest desires?

This need for speed leaves us feeling in a hurry to receive our definition of success almost instantly. As the villain agitates the hero, impatience, bitterness, and comparison kick in. This results in reactive behavior.[9] Meaning, actions grounded in lack, scarcity, or fear, driven by a short-term mindset. The result? Transactional behavior that prevents people from building trusted relationships.

CONSIDER THIS

How many times have you seen someone achieve explosive business growth, but sacrifice their people along the way?

How many times have you seen someone land a coveted C-suite role, but sacrifice their integrity along the way?

How many times have you seen someone go viral on social media, but sacrifice their authenticity along the way?

The result? Emptiness, a loss of identity, and a bunch of nine-year-olds who liked your cat video on social but can't afford your services.

Okay, I joke, but you see where I'm coming from, right?

When we engage in short-term behavior, things get ugly. Ugly as in:

- Creating "fake urgency" with a prospect so you can shorten your sales cycle and land that big commission check.
- Sprinkling fairy dust on your numbers when presenting your progress to leadership, partners, or investors, to maintain your image.
- Masking the realities around a compensation plan to fill an open position as quickly as possible and hit quota.
- Rallying your team around a vision that solely serves your bank balance at their personal and professional expense.
- Sabotaging another team member's character by using them as a scapegoat for unsatisfactory business outcomes to protect your own reputation.

Not only do these short-term behaviors ensure you're out of integrity with others, but they'll guarantee that you're out of integrity with yourself. Our villain, when roaming free within the four walls of our mind, has the power to dilute relationship currency almost instantly. How have we gotten to a place where operating from a place of integrity has become a path to standing out?

As the world entices you to swim in a pool of automation (without intimacy), to scale (without reason), and to always seek more (without purpose), staying afloat requires deep awareness. Yes, this requires conscious effort, a deconditioning from society's norms, and a "contrarian" approach. But just know: you've officially been granted the permission to own your value system and rid yourself of the pressure to conform.

When all is said and done, you'll become a symbol for others, showing them what's possible when you transform yourself into an influential communicator. However, before we get into it, I need to ensure we're on the same page about the word "influence."

OUR VEHICLE FOR TRANSFORMATION: COMMUNICATING WITH INFLUENCE

In today's digital age, when most people hear the term "influence," they instantly associate it with being an "influencer" or use it interchangeably with "manipulation." The "influencer" label is often met with resistance. Some see it as a path to building a movement around their mission, while others view it as an opportunity to make a quick buck by promoting or selling products and services with no intrinsic value. I'll let you decide which side of the fence you sit on.

Interestingly, if we look at the word influence, from the Latin word *influere*, meaning "to flow in," it dates back to the fourteenth century and has nothing to do with selling anything; it had an early astrological meaning. "Celestial bodies were thought to have 'influence'; meaning, an ethereal fluid flowed from the heavens and affected the destiny of humans." It wasn't until the mid-1600s that the word "influence" was attached to groups or individuals and their ability to affect others' belief systems.[10]

Now, if we look at the current definition of influence, according to *Oxford Learner's Dictionaries*, it is "The effect that somebody/something has on the way a person thinks or behaves or on the way that something works or develops."[11] While this interpretation does speak to me, I can't help but feel like it's missing one word: positive. That is, "The [positive] effect that somebody/something ..." In a nutshell, this is exactly what I'm about. Helping you increase your capacity to have a positive effect on those around you and doing so with integrity.

For me, our good old friend integrity is the key difference between influence and manipulation. To unpack this further, I'm talking about having positive intent and ensuring an abundant outcome for the person you want to serve. This ensures you're rooted in integrity.

Sure, this is my truth, but here's a universal truth for you: helping others get more of what they desire is intrinsically good, as long as the consequence isn't harmful to oneself or others. When we transform our day-to-day communication into influential communication, we instantly boost our ability to build trusted relationships. When done right, you won't play a zero-sum game. Meaning, you won't seek to gain at another human being's expense. Ultimately, abundance will find you when you communicate with influence versus manipulation.

Let's walk through an example that might be close to home. Picture this: you're on a call with Jennifer, a senior decision-maker and potential buyer of your solution. She's in the initial stages of deciding whether you can solve her problem and improve her company's marketing strategy as they look to increase buyer intent among US millennials. Through the art of asking conscious questions and deep listening (which we will cover in Habit 2), you end up having a meaningful conversation that matters.

As you dig deeper, it turns out that your solution isn't the right fit for Jennifer. As you seek to influence, not manipulate, you walk through your diagnosis and prescribe an alternative service that doesn't benefit your bank balance. And because you operated with integrity, you're able to accelerate trust in the budding relationship. While your sales numbers didn't change that day, Jennifer's life did. The very solution you introduced her to ended up being a perfect fit for her company and landed her a promotion. Eighteen months later, you receive a referral via email leading to the biggest deal of your career. The source: Jennifer.

When you have positive intent and seek an abundant outcome for the person you're looking to serve, you don't allow reactive behavior to auto-enroll you as a player in a zero-sum game. Consequentially, you are rooted in nothing but integrity. Do this right and abundance will find you. Maybe not in the time frame or through a path you expected, but it will find you. This example is a reminder that trust is the cornerstone of any and every relationship.

THE THREE C'S OF TRUST (CONNECTION, CHARACTER, & COMPETENCE)

Trust has become an elusive buzzword overused by politicians, marketers, and brands, often rooted in virtue signaling. Don't get it twisted; the problem doesn't lie in one's use of the word. It lies in one's inability to walk their talk. According to a *2024 Edelman Trust Barometer Global Report*,[12] 61 percent of respondents worry that business leaders are purposely trying to mislead people by communicating things that are false or exaggerated. A lack of congruency is fatal, and it's why we are facing a global trust recession.

In order to demystify this term, I've traveled back in time to identify the moments in my life where I've been able to build trust prolifically, and lose it in a similar fashion. As I went down this rabbit hole, the answer slapped me in the face like a wet fish. What

I'm about to show you isn't a formula, blueprint, or universal truth. It's an intuitive set of variables derived from my lived experience (a.k.a. my truth).

Allow me to introduce you to the Three C's of Trust: connection, character, and competence. Let's break it down.

Connection is the emotional glue that helps us forge a meaningful bond with another human being. This can be developed through habits that spark intimacy, such as the stories we tell, the questions we ask, how we listen, and the energy we exude. When done right, this and more can help us create high levels of affinity with another human being. (We'll discuss this more in Habits 2, 3, and 4.)

Character concerns the visible and invisible values that travel with one's verbal and non-verbal communication, allowing others to consciously and subconsciously uncover what we stand for. You'll see these themes play out across all of the learnings that lie ahead.

Competence revolves around another human being's perception of your expertise, which can increase or decrease your credibility stock. Our ability to signal competence without shoving it down somebody's throat is critical in any conversation, meeting, or presentation. (More on this later, too.)

Here's the conundrum: Being able to connect with another person may get you through the front door, but if your values portray you as somebody of poor character, the emotional glue that stuck that relationship together will instantly disintegrate. However, even if your character does stand the test of time and the relationship does see some growth, if you can't signal competence and deliver your expertise in a way that gives them the keys to their kingdom, the river in that relationship will run dry, and your perceived credibility will plummet. Given you're reading this book, I don't need to tell you that true expertise is table stakes.

On the other hand, relying on competence alone may get you what you desire in the near term, but this can result in a transactional relationship that lacks depth and meaning. This leads to an absence of loyalty, and the moment you're seen as a commodity, you become easily disposable. The trifecta of connection, character, and competence is required alongside one another for longevity, especially when we're discussing your ability to sell yourself, an idea, vision, product, or service. Regardless of our title, label, or whether we like to admit it or not, everybody is in sales.

Here's the punchline: connection and character, or competence alone, can get you through the front door, but without all three performing in unison, the probability of you building a long-lasting relationship is slim.

Soon, we'll go on to explore the five habits of communicating with influence, and you'll see how you can spark connection, showcase your character, and signal competence, so you can build trusted relationships that last. However, to hammer this home and paint a vivid picture of what this looks like in practice, I'll hit you with a personal example of the Three C's and how they helped me land an internship opportunity that changed the trajectory of my life.

THE THREE C'S OF TRUST IN PRACTICE

As I hit adulthood, I decided I wanted to live life in the fast lane. I thought sharp suits, a slick car, and a big paycheck were my ticket to fulfillment. How was I going to do it? By landing a sales job on the trading floor at one of the largest investment banks in the world. As Gordon Gekko, Michael Douglas's character in the movie *Wall Street* once said, "Greed is good." And I was all in. Whoever had the keys to my kingdom, I was going to find them.

At the time, there was an unwritten rule that top-tier banks only hired graduates from target institutions. Very quickly, it became clear that my undergraduate degree in economics at Sheffield University wasn't going to cut it. I was committed to the vision, so the moment I graduated, I immediately enrolled to study for a master's degree in banking and international finance at Cass Business School (now Bayes Business School).

Oh, and did I mention the year was 2010 and we were knee-deep in the aftermath of the global financial crisis? Banks had collapsed, economic turmoil was at its highest, and the job market was volatile. Yet, I was enthusiastic, deluded, and most importantly, naive.

Job application after job application led to rejection email after rejection email, and I wasn't the only one experiencing this. Fewer than three people out of my entire postgraduate class had landed a full-time job, and things looked ugly. Word on the street was that applying for graduate jobs was a fool's game. What you wanted to do was apply for a summer internship, which was the gateway to almost all graduate hiring. This was the light bulb moment I didn't know I needed. I decided to remove my ego and delay gratification as I went on a rampage of applying for summer internships.

The result? Crickets. My inbox was silent, and my resume and cover letter weren't seeing the light of day. No face time with a hiring manager meant zero chance for connection. A jargon-filled cover letter meant zero chance for showcasing my character. And with my resume exhibiting little to no social proof of my ability to play at the highest level, there was zero chance of me signaling competence. Giving up wasn't an option, but my morale was at an all-time low. All I needed was an opportunity to build trust through a meaningful conversation with another human being. Little did I know, an unexpected gift was heading my way.

"Barclays Capital will be coming into our class next week to deliver a presentation. Three members of their Credit Risk Department (two directors and a recent graduate) are going to walk you through what it's like to work at the bank, share what it takes to succeed, and answer your questions. Make sure nobody's late!" My professor had just handed me a golden ticket. I was Charlie, and she was Willy Wonka . . . could this be THE unexpected path to meet my burning desire?

I knew I didn't want to work in credit risk, but I also knew this could be a stepping stone to everything I thought I desired. *Could this be the moment that changes everything?*

The morning of the talk, I picked up the *Financial Times*, inhaled it, and scribbled down a few thoughtful and research-driven questions. I had one thing on my mind: How can I stand out in a sea of graduates who all looked, sounded, and behaved exactly the same?

After a brief presentation from the team at Barclays, I finally heard the words I'd been waiting for, "Does anybody have any questions?" This was it! I leaned back in my chair, fiddled with my bag strap, and watched my hands produce buckets of sweat as I tried to figure out the perfect time to raise one of them. Question after question went by. I'd use one word to describe them: vanilla. After three or four questions from my peers, I decided it was game time, and I raised my hand.

"Yes, you there at the back?"

My first question caught their attention, built rapport, and sparked a two-way dialogue. I felt the energy start to shift in the room. But it was my next question that changed the game.

"Given the scrutiny this morning around Barclays's Universal Banking model, if abandoned, what impact do you feel this would have on the profitability of your investment banking operations?"

Heads turned, and there was a moment of pin-drop silence. This was the pattern interrupt I was hoping for.

In that moment, a genuine connection began to form.

"Erm, haha, I'm not sure how to answer that if I'm honest!" said one of the directors, as they all chuckled to themselves.

Boom. Just like that, my in-depth morning research led to me asking a series of conscious questions (we'll discuss this in Habit 2) that told them a positive story about my character. And using industry terminology gave my questions a level of depth that signaled competence. Even more importantly, it wasn't just about what I said, but *how* I said it. The voice tools earned and the lessons learned from performing in theater were working their magic.

During the networking drinks, I knew I had paved the way for a meaningful conversation. As I walked over to introduce myself to the team at Barclays, I was instantly met with warmth, and more importantly, curiosity. Admittedly, I wasn't the most academically gifted in my class, but that day, I was able to do something that nobody else could: build trust.

By the end of that conversation, I was invited to apply for a summer internship in the Credit Risk Department and was fast-tracked to the interview process. After a grueling day of interviews and group exercises, I was offered a paid summer internship in 2011.

This internship at Barclays was a piece to the puzzle that helped me launch my brief career in banking. In 2013, I began a full-time role as a corporate salesperson on the trading floor at Citibank (through the gateway of a summer internship may I add). Mission accomplished.

As I look back and unravel the bigger picture, here's how I see it (hindsight is a beautiful thing). Through the art of communication, I was able to tap into my limitless influence, build trust, and forge a meaningful bond. The result? The opportunity of a lifetime for my former self. As the team at Barclays gave me the keys to my kingdom, I also gave them a set of keys to theirs by helping them hire an intern who didn't sound or operate like their other candidates, allowing me to earn true relationship currency. By delaying gratification and welcoming a summer internship in an unexpected department of the business, I walked an unforeseen path toward my ultimate desire.

Now, before we immerse ourselves into the five communication habits, let me give you a preview of what to expect from the remainder of this book.

SNEAK PEEK: THE FIVE COMMUNICATION HABITS

This book is designed to help you supercharge your ability to master the art of communication, tap into your limitless influence, and build trusted relationships that unlock your desires, without violating your values.

You'll learn how to:

- Transform your internal story, so you can crack open the limiting belief that's preventing you from communicating with authenticity.
- Ask conscious questions and deeply listen, so you can build rapport, exude intentionality, and prevent transactional conversations.
- Unearth your charisma, without being self-centered, and make others feel significant in your presence, so you can spark intimacy, connection, and loyalty.
- Become a magnetic storyteller who is able to gain buy-in for their vision, ideas, products, or services effortlessly without being pushy.

- Communicate like a trusted guide, so you can signal competence, increase your credibility stock, and build business relationships that last a lifetime.

There *is* a method to this madness. If you skip ahead, approach each habit looking for a magic bullet, or don't take imperfect action, you'll do your future self a disservice. Going through this book in the exact sequence laid out and implementing as you go is where the magic lies.

Before we continue, I need you to know this. Earning relationship currency requires a detachment from your desire and a focus on one question: How can I give somebody the keys to their kingdom without the expectation of reciprocity?

The key to building meaningful relationships with others first begins with building an intimate relationship with yourself and uncovering the current story that is ruling your internal world. That's exactly where we're heading next.

As Anthony told little Ravi just before the big dance recital, it's showtime!

TRANSFORM YOUR INTERNAL STORY

You are the stories you tell yourself.

No tactics, strategies, or frameworks will help you truly communicate with influence unless you're invested in a journey of introspection. For some, that could mean engaging in a journaling or meditation practice; for others that may mean having reflective conversations with a therapist, mentor, coach, or friend, where it feels safe to be vulnerable. I invite you to be flexible in your modality of choice, yet fixed on the following belief: the inner work makes the dream work.

As you begin your journey, you'll uncover one beautiful, yet painful, truth: you are the stories you tell yourself. These stories unconsciously shape your inner world, creating the lens through which you view the outer world, but more importantly, yourself. But here's the problem, some of these stories are secretly suffocating your ability to become an effective, authentic, and influential communicator. If the habits in this book are designed to accelerate your success, but your internal story simultaneously has the parking brake on, you'll travel nowhere fast.

In my own experience, the result of a lifelong commitment to doing the inner work is becoming increasingly comfortable in your own skin. The more comfortable you are in yourself, the more potent you become as a communicator. So, this habit is about saying "yes" to exploring your inner world, beginning with the path of transforming your internal story.

To be clear, the practice shared in this chapter is a starting point, not an endpoint. Once again, I invite you to identify a source of support to help you while you discover and alleviate the root cause of the stories that could be sabotaging your growth. The more you discover about yourself, unpack the beliefs that are holding you back, and uncover the associated stories that are dimming your light, the more your personal relationship with authenticity will grow. And not only will you become an influential communicator, but you'll become unapologetically self-expressed.

Remember, if you want to learn how to build trusted relationships with others, the first human being you need to befriend is yourself. Do this right and you'll begin to upgrade your identity and become the type of person who's able to receive and sustain their deepest desires.

Let's get into it!

INFLUENCING YOURSELF (AND OTHERS)

For the first six-ish months of our daughter's life, my wife and I were unknowingly dedicated to increasing the share price of Deliveroo, a service that delivers restaurant-ready food to your door in rapid time. Every single evening, we'd open our fridge door, feast our eyes on a host of fresh food ready to be cooked, and slowly look at each other with nothing but shame.

The perceived effort of making a home-cooked meal was too high, and within minutes, our sleep-deprived brains decided to take the (privileged) path of least resistance and order a meal from our favorite restaurant through Deliveroo. This decision was unfavorable for our bank balance, far from rational, and allowed our villain of instant gratification to win the day. So why did we do it? Because we are emotional beings, living in an irrational world, engaging in an imperfect human experience that we call life.

Dr. Zoe Chance, senior lecturer at Yale School of Management,[13] believes every human being has a "gator" and "judge" within them, otherwise known as "system 1" and "system 2," according to behavioral economists. The gator—an alligator—is the fast, intuitive, and unconscious part of our brain that drives up to 95 percent of our decision-making. This is the home where our emotions live. The judge is like a judge in court, slow, deliberate, and conscious as they carefully weigh up evidence before making a rational decision. The gator is automatic; the judge requires effort, and funny enough, the former is considerably more dominant.

Zoe sees the gator as the master gatekeeper and the first responder who filters and influences what information you pay attention to in the first place. This results in you automatically using the gator to make nearly all your decisions on a day-to-day basis. Yes, the judge processes factual information, analytical data, and more, but interestingly, what it's doing behind the scenes is rationalizing the preferences of the emotional gator. Ultimately, we humans are prone to taking the path of least resistance and prioritizing ease.[14]

Returning to my wife and I in front of the open fridge: "Should we order takeout, or should we cook a healthy meal from scratch?"

As new parents who value our health, this was the "tough" question that plagued our minds daily. Here's how I see it: When we were irritable and overwhelmed, without even blinking, we would place an online order just like that. Meaning that when we were hanging on by a thread, and at our most hungry and fatigued, our gator within would take control of the steering wheel and order takeout, as that felt like an easy decision to make. Interestingly, when we had a good night's sleep and felt energized, we would make the conscious decision to cook a meal at home, even though it was more effort and took longer, because we had more decision-making fuel in our tank. The bottom line is this: as much as we human beings like to believe we are rational and logical most of the time, that's far from the truth.

As you'll learn throughout this book, when influencing others, it's extremely important to prioritize the needs of their gators, before appealing to the wants of their judges. This requires you to establish an emotional connection and spark curiosity instead of leading with facts and figures. Once you open the hearts of the people you're trying to impact, you'll earn the chance to appeal to their minds so you can influence with integrity.

So, what now? When it comes to transforming yourself into an influential communicator, it doesn't begin with snackable method-ologies, strategies, and frameworks. It starts by delaying gratifica-tion and consciously putting forth the effort to understand what you believe about yourself as a communicator, the emotive story attached to this belief, and rewiring it for success. Then and only then can we spark true change within ourselves, and thus, others.

YOU ARE A PRODUCT OF YOUR BELIEFS

The books you consume (including this one). The movies you watch. The friends you keep. The family you have. The environment you live in. The mentors you turn to. The place in which you work—the list goes on. All of these people, places, things, and more are secretly influencing—or manipulating—you every single day, even if you don't realize it.

Each of these vehicles is "a messenger," spreading information and sparking an emotion within. If we break it down, the word "emotion" simply means "energy in motion." As I see it, certain information will trigger an emotional charge, producing energy that'll travel through your body and pick up speed as external messengers continue to reinforce this piece of information.

The manifestation of this process is a set of internal beliefs and, thus, stories you tell yourself. These stories operate as a launchpad for all of your behaviors. When repeated consistently, a portion of these behaviors will turn into habits that run your life on autopilot. According to psychologist Wendy Wood, approximately "43 percent of what people do every day is repeated in the same context," normally while they are thinking about something else.[15] As I see it, Chance's analogy of the gator and the judge support and illustrate Woods's point: we are automatically responding (leading with the gator), without really making any conscious decisions (utilizing the judge).

Let me hit you with an example to illustrate my point. I am the son of two immigrant parents who made their way from Africa to the UK when they were youngsters. "Your dad arrived without a penny in his pocket," as my mum loves to say. Yet, by the age of thirty-two, he was one of the youngest partners at professional services firm PricewaterhouseCoopers. Happily retired and enjoying life as a grandfather, my dad still tells me to this day how much he enjoyed his thirty-five years at the firm.

Growing up, I observed my dad receive deep fulfillment and joy from his career, sparking an emotion of excitement within me about the endless possibilities if I, too, carved out my own path in corporate. However, my dad wasn't the only one proud of his illustrious career. Growing up, society's definition of success and the way the rest of my family celebrated him for living out the immigrant dream were the first "messengers" to reinforce an automatic and subconscious belief: I am destined for a career in corporate.

As time went on, this unknowingly manifested into the following story: "The only way to achieve success is by climbing the corporate ladder," which became a launchpad for all of my behaviors, and thus, habits. Without any conscious decision-making, my work experience, my university degree of choice, and the mentors I looked up to all pointed toward pursuing a path in corporate.

And I did it, remember? I landed my dream job at Citibank on the trading floor back in early 2013. Here's what I didn't tell you: I resigned after just three and a half years. See, on paper, I had everything I desired. But I was secretly craving a deeper sense of purpose that my corporate career wasn't offering me. My desires had evolved, and I was on the wrong path to reach them. Yet, I was holding on to my original internal story with a death grip.

This resulted in hundreds of hours of planning the perfect exit strategy and countless coffee conversations with other hopeful corporate escapees, where I complained about my dilemma only to find myself doing nothing about it. The resistance and dissonance were real, and this went on for months on end. My inaction was due to my internal belief and associated story, which was subconsciously governing my behavior. The question that remained was this: Who was Ravi if he no longer believed he was destined for a high-flying corporate career and wasn't perceived by the external world as "living the dream"? My intuition was screaming at me to leave, yet I consistently silenced it. Until I didn't.

In August of 2016, I resigned and began what I now call "the Great Experiment." This included four years of testing various career paths, such as TV presenting, coaching, fractional consulting, and sales leadership in tech, until I went all in on entrepreneurship in September 2020. This is where my journey of teaching others the art of communication officially began. It turns out that success will find you when you redefine it, question your internal story (more on this shortly), and remain open to the path to receiving your ever-evolving desires. Transforming my internal story wasn't an overnight process; in hindsight, it was a lesson in delayed gratification.

My story aside, let's talk about you. What narratives have you been told or sold, and are holding on to that are sabotaging or accelerating your success? The answer lies in first identifying the beliefs that drive the stories you tell yourself.

YOUR INTERNAL BELIEFS: LABELING

If you walk into your kitchen and open the nearest cupboard, you'll see a sea of jars, packets, and condiments with labels on them. If you examine one of them, you'll likely see a brand logo, a product name, a list of ingredients, and more. The goal is to ensure the identity of this product is focused, clear, and most importantly, fixed. Intuitively, a label in this context makes sense, right?

However, applying a singular label to human beings to fix their identity is not only problematic but dangerous. On one hand, labeling ourselves can give us a sense of identity, confidence, and belonging. Sounds great, right? But on the other hand, fixing our identity can cause us to think small, develop self-limiting beliefs, and engage in behaviors to protect the label we've adopted. The words we use to define ourselves influence our behavior and shift the trajectory of our lives.

Labeling is a theory first developed by Howard Becker in 1963. In his body of work, he speaks about the harmful effects of labels on children. For example, have you ever heard a parent say, "My son is extremely bossy" or "She's very shy"? To a child, these words carry weight, meaning, and significance. Becker proposed that labels can influence how a child views themselves, leading to a self-fulfilling prophecy. Consistently labeling a child as "bossy" or "shy," due to them showing such tendencies in a prior season of their life, could mean they end up engaging in behaviors that are congruent with this label. Becker's thesis implies that children are developing and have endless potential, so we shouldn't suffocate this process with well-intentioned yet harmful labels.[16] I believe the same holds for you and me as adults. We are limitless beings, but things get dicey when a label consumes your entire identity. I've seen and heard clients use the following labels to describe themselves when it comes to their communication:

- Boring
- Monotone
- Uncharismatic
- Uninspiring
- Ineffective

The list could go on—do any of the above resonate?

I once had a client who was in-between sales jobs in the tech industry. After "bombing" a best man speech (his words) many years before, he labeled himself "a bad presenter." This label became a part of his identity as a communicator, stimulating self-limiting beliefs and stunting his career potential. The result? His teammates would avoid giving him the spotlight in high-stakes pitches. His leaders didn't acknowledge his hard-earned expertise because of his inability to articulate his message. And his peers didn't view him as influential. This impacted how he saw himself, reinforcing behaviors congruent with the label he had adopted.

But don't get it twisted: even so-called "positive" labels can be destructive.

For example, I recently delivered a storytelling workshop in the UK. One individual in the group had proudly given themselves the label of being "confident." The problem was that their interpretation of this label meant they believed they should display unconscious competence in every single area of their life. When I presented the group with a fresh take on customer-centric conversations using influential storytelling, this individual resisted it at all costs. Why? They didn't want to admit that their current conversations could be improved. They didn't want to engage in practice and be seen as a beginner in front of their peers. And they didn't want to showcase any vulnerability, as for them, that was the opposite of confidence.

As a result, they disengaged with the session, shied away from asking questions, and became disinterested. They told themself, "This won't work for me." When the leadership team and I dug deeper, the proof was in the pudding. This individual was engaging in behaviors to protect the label they had given themself. Their label and definition of "confident" were preventing them from refining their skills, having better customer conversations, and earning relationship currency in their industry. Positive or negative, the question is how can we reframe a label into something that serves us?

In the most basic sense, the shift lies in one word: verbs. Instead of pinning your entire identity on a singular noun, use a verb (a.k.a. an action word) to expand your being and belief system. For instance, in the case of the example above, instead of saying, "I am confident," one could say, "I am a lifelong learner who *displays deep competence* in my area of expertise." Instead of saying, "I am a bad presenter," one could say, "I am someone who is consistently growing in my skills as a presenter." Nonetheless, no matter how long a label, belief, or story has been plaguing you, just know, change is always possible.

TRANSFORMING THE STORIES YOU TELL YOURSELF

As you know by now, my parents had a flare for enrolling me into life-changing extracurricular activities. This time was no different; however, instead of dance class, it was swimming lessons. Now, I wasn't going to be the next Michael Phelps, but I had a little something something going on. It was enough for Lori, the co-owner and teacher of the swim school, to invite me to participate in Saturday afternoon's advanced group. But the problem was their swimming pool felt like the depths of the Antarctic Ocean. My body shivered, and my teeth chattered even thinking about the temperature of that pool!

Every Saturday morning, I woke up with a sick feeling in my stomach, dreading the afternoon lesson. After my breakfast, I would immediately begin devising the perfect master plan to ensure Lori would have no choice but to put a cross next to my name on the attendance register. But my parents had other plans. They were wise to my weekly performance, and no excuse ever qualified as valid. Just like dance class, I had to go.

As a father to two children now myself, I'm incredibly grateful that my parents had the resources and desire to have me try so many different sports and activities. Funny enough, it wasn't until very recently that I uncovered one of those sports—swimming—as the source of a label, belief, and story that has stuck with me since I was a skinny little Indian kid. The self-imposed label? My immune system is weak. The belief? The cold isn't good for you; it makes you sick. The story? I hate the cold. Whether it was a winter walk with my dog, breathing in fresh cold air in the morning, or traveling to a beautiful (colder) part of the world, for as long as I can remember, I disliked it with a passion. Fast forward to 2023, and I was finally ready to transform my story.

Every single time I logged on to social media, I saw a sea of people who labeled themselves as elite athletes, entrepreneurs, and high performers engaging in cold plunging. Initially, I rolled my eyes and judged what I thought was a fad. However, as supporting "messengers" consistently reinforced the benefits of cold-water immersion, my ears perked up, and an emotion of wonder began to slowly spark within. As this "energy in motion" began to manifest, I started to question myself: Do I really have weak immunity? Will the cold truly make me sick? Do I actually hate the cold?

At the time, I was a first-time father to a one-year-old and wanted to bolster my immune system to ensure it was battle-ready for the sickness bugs coming my way from our daughter's daycare. But beneath the surface, this desire was rooted in my core motivation to become a more impactful father, husband, and leader. As they say, "Health is wealth," and I was all in, with cold plunging being one of many paths to receiving my desire. In September 2023, I decided enough was enough, and I secretly committed to the following identity: I am someone who cold plunges. No passive language here, I was totally invested, and my Amazon order history proved it. My inner child, the cheap cold plunge tub I had just purchased, and I were ready to take on the world.

The moment it came, fear slapped me in the face harder than Will Smith at the Oscars. Nope, I didn't unwrap the package like a kid at Christmas. Quite the contrary. Instead, I quietly slid the package into my office and let it gather dust. For the following few weeks, my internal story dominated my external behavior and prevented me from forming a new habit. But on one fine day in October, I was sick and tired of negotiating with myself. It was time to ignite change.

From that Saturday afternoon onwards, I began deliberate, gradual, and intentional cold plunging. My first-ever plunge was at sixty-eight degrees Fahrenheit. Nothing to shout about—my wife even heckled me, calling it lukewarm bathwater—but I still remember the moment I hopped out. I felt like a superhero dammit! The skinny Indian boy within me who winced at the cold was fist pumping the air. Let's go!

And then, the very next day, reality struck. I woke up with a headache and a cold. My mind instantly said, "See, I told you it was gonna make you sick," but it didn't matter. I was committed to shifting my internal story and falling in love with the cold. Regardless of this minor bump in the road, a transformation was brewing. I was officially someone who cold plunged, and now, all I needed was the consistency required to build momentum. If the next version of me is somebody who embodies this habit, shouldn't I start behaving like this human being today? To collapse time on my transformation, I decided to begin operating like Ravi 2.0 immediately. Instead of faking it till you make it, I began acting as if and stayed true to the process.

The story I had told myself my entire life was beginning to crack. Why? The more I plunged, the more evidence I collected to prove I have a strong immune system. The more I plunged, the more I proved myself wrong: the cold doesn't make you sick. The more I plunged, the more I identified with my newfound story of being somebody who enjoys the cold. Fast forward to today . . . I consistently cold plunge at temperatures that would give Lori's swim school pool a run for its money. After all this time, I still don't see myself going back on this habit. Sure, many critics believe the benefits of cold water immersion are a myth. However, here's my truth: I feel superhuman every single time I get out of my cold plunge. I feel an increase in my vitality, energy, and dopamine levels—even if it's a placebo—from doing the HARD thing. But more importantly, I consistently disown the story that subconsciously ruled little Ravi's mind every Saturday morning before swim class. And that is good enough for me. Today, I can safely say I am someone who enjoys the cold.

Here's why this matters to our conversation: Can you imagine the subtle shifts that occur when you crack open the stories that aren't serving you and embody the mindset and communication habits of the future you?

Things like your body language, presence, aura, posture, confidence, and more will all begin to map toward the version of you that communicates with influence and has already received their desires. So, where do we begin? Enter the ten-step process for transforming your internal communication story.

PRACTICE: THE TEN-STEP PROCESS TO TRANSFORM YOUR INTERNAL STORY

What I'm about to share is loosely based on a private client of mine who was a leader at a fast-growing tech company. Let's call him Ryan. On the surface, Ryan's challenge was the art of communication. The C-suite didn't put him forward for external speaking opportunities, he struggled to tell concise stories under pressure, and his peers told him that he wasn't doing his incredible expertise justice. Once we dug deeper, it was clear that communicating with influence wasn't the core problem; it was a niggling story that was ruling Ryan's internal world and sabotaging his external results.

Unknowingly, Ryan had adopted a label throughout his entire career that was crushing his ability to gain buy-in for his ideas, inspire action in his team, and achieve more fulfillment in his career. It was time to transform Ryan's associated internal story for communication success. Here's a refined version of the process we used in action, with ten powerful steps at the heart of the transformation:

STEP 1: What is ONE consistent label that you have adopted throughout your career?

(The goal is to identify a label that you have [consciously or subconsciously] adopted which has left you playing small in your career or business.)

I am a "techie."

STEP 2: What do you believe about people (or yourself) who define themselves by this exact label?

(The goal is to be honest with yourself and uncover your beliefs attached to this label without judgement.)

Techies (like me) are too detail oriented, boring, and are unable to communicate their message articulately. We are better and more comfortable when operating behind the scenes.

STEP 3: What's one story that you tell yourself due to this belief?

(The goal is to reveal the internal story that has molded your current reality.)

> *I'm a technical leader who isn't a clear, engaging, or confident communicator.*

STEP 4: How long have you believed this story?

(The goal is to help you acknowledge and quantify how long you've been governed by this internal story.)

> *For over twenty-three years! It all began after my first-ever manager told me I struggle to communicate my ideas in meetings and that clients find my communication style confusing.*

STEP 5: What is it costing you (professionally and personally) to hold on to this story?

(The goal is to qualitatively understand what it will cost you if you don't make change and take imperfect action.)

> *Professionally: More fulfillment in my career and the ability to be seen as a transformational leader among my team, leadership, and peers.*
> *Personally: Achieving financial prosperity, supporting my family, and living the lifestyle of our dreams without regret.*

STEP 6: Is this story 100 percent true?

(The goal is for you to reflect and find a piece of evidence that proves this internal story wrong. Even if it creates the tiniest of cracks in your story's validity, we're on the right track.)

No, this story isn't 100 percent true. Two years ago, after delivering a presentation at our company kick-off, I was told by our CEO that when I'm firing on all cylinders, I am a clear, open, engaging, and high-energy public speaker.

STEP 7: Transform the story that isn't serving you into one that excites you, sparks a positive emotion, and maps to the version of you that's already received their desires.

(The goal is for you to use exciting words that ignite new energy within, ensuring you use specific language that's rooted in the present tense rather than future tense. Why? Remember, we want to collapse time and begin behaving like the future you, today.)

Old story: *I am a technical leader who isn't a clear, engaging, or confident communicator.*
New story: *I am a technical leader with world-class expertise, who communicates with powerful precision, radical authenticity, and unshakable confidence.*

STEP 8: What's one behavior you can engage in, in the next twenty-four hours to support this new story?

(The goal is to decrease the distance from thought to execution, begin building momentum, and collect positive evidence to increase your belief in your new story.)

As they say, "We can't be what we can't see." I'm going to find and watch a highly successful TED talk delivered by a "technical" thought leader who's able to inspire the masses to prove this is possible!

STEP 9: How will you collect supporting evidence daily to anchor your new story over the next thirty days?

(The goal is to ensure we create momentum and consistently stack new evidence to strengthen your new internal story, so you can develop a habit of reverting to a positive set of reference points that center you when self-doubt creeps in.)

I will engage in a video challenge, where every single day for thirty days, I will share a sixty-second story on camera and have it reviewed by my accountability partner at work for feedback.

STEP 10: When your old story rears its ugly head, what practice will you use to ground yourself in your new story?

(As you commit to your new internal story, old patterns will resurface. This is welcomed, as it is part of the cleansing process and an opportunity for you to reconnect with the new narrative. The goal is to feel the discomfort without resistance, allow it to pass through you, and find a modality that helps you ground yourself in your desired reality.)

Rewatching my favorite snippet from the TED talk I found and watched, and meditating for five minutes to help me regulate my nervous system.

In my work with Ryan, we didn't begin with storytelling, public speaking, and communication tactics. We began with the inner work, and this was the foundation of Ryan's transformation. Not only did he go on to deliver a successful virtual talk in front of hundreds of employees at his company, but he began to shift how others saw him. And more importantly, he shifted how he saw himself. Instead of trying to imitate his peers, colleagues, or mentors, he developed the confidence to own his unique energy and embody a communication style that felt authentic to him. His desire: to feel valued professionally. His path: transforming his internal story. Mission accomplished.

If you're looking to try these ten steps on for size for yourself or your team, head over to theravirajani.com/bookresources to grab your one-page worksheet.

YOUR HIDDEN STORY: TREATING THE ROOT CAUSE

At the top of this habit, do you remember when I invited you to embrace the belief that the inner work makes the dream work? As some of you complete this practice yourself, you may feel inspired to continue your journey of introspection using an external modality of your choice. For example, a coach, mentor, therapist, or friend you connect with, believe to be of great character, and who has elite competence; meaning somebody you deeply trust.

This is an opportunity to identify and alleviate the root cause of your internal story (also known as a "hidden story"), which has prevented you from being a masterful communicator. As you go beneath the surface, you may realize that this hidden story has secretly kept you from having a career, business, and life of abundance. For example, a hidden story of "I am not enough," could be causing you to not speak up in meetings, engage in unhealthy comparison, shrink your personal desires, or engage in people-pleasing behavior that suffocates your true voice. The list is endless.

Know that by treating the root cause, you will walk the road less traveled. There may be a breakdown before a breakthrough, but remember this: personal growth lies in your ability to get comfortable with being uncomfortable. Yes, I want you to honor where you're at in this season of your life. No, you don't need to be "fixed." And yes, you are enough exactly as you are. However, there's another level of abundance waiting for you, in business and life.

WHY THIS MATTERS: WHEN PROFESSIONAL GROWTH OVERSHADOWS PERSONAL GROWTH

"Ravi, can't I skip this woo-woo stuff and just hustle my way to my desires?" You are the king or queen of your kingdom, my friend, and you may do as you please. However, think about it like this. Imagine owning a new smartphone only to find it's running on an older operating system. Slow performance. Security threats. And that's just the tip of the iceberg. This is no different to claiming a new desire while refusing to upgrade your identity. To receive, keep, and grow your external desires, upgrading your internal software is essential. Here's a case in point.

In a different season of my life, I knew a founder and CEO of an early-stage tech startup. Their genius was nothing like I'd seen before. They were the type of leader who could transform a vision into a viable business at lightning speed, with product excellence at the center of their universe.

Over the years, as their business began to pick up steam, their professional growth was something to admire from afar, but up close, from my own lens, there was little to no emphasis on personal growth. As they raised capital, began scaling, and pursued a path for industry domination, something interesting occurred. The connection with their employees appeared to have stalled, their character came into question, and their competence began to show cracks. The result? An absence of the Three C's and a trust deficit across their entire organization. As I saw it, the business had outgrown the identity of its leader. And eventually, this, among many other contributing factors, led to a demise of their business in rapid fashion. Here's why this matters to you, my friend: taking the time to explore your inner world is critical for deep, meaningful, and long-term success in business. This will ensure that your identity is a match for your desires and that as those desires evolve, you do too.

As we get tactical in the next chapter on how to ask conscious questions that unlock connection, remember this: the depth of your relationships with others is a direct reflection of the depth of the relationship you have with yourself. The best way to achieve depth? Meaningful questions that matter. In this habit, you began asking yourself meaningful questions through the ten-step process for transforming your internal story. In Habit 2, you'll learn how to ask meaningful questions to others so you can build business relationships that last a lifetime.

THE HIGHLIGHT REEL

1. Earning the trust of others begins with building trust in yourself.

2. Labels can be dangerous, creating a mental cage of beliefs that limit your abundance, influence, and growth.

3. The stories you tell yourself are a launchpad for your behaviors and, consequentially, habits that you unknowingly engage in daily.

4. Uncovering the internal story that's preventing you from communicating with influence is one thing. But treating the root cause, a.k.a. the "hidden story," is where true change lies.

5. In order to receive, keep, and grow your desires, you must upgrade your internal operating system, a.k.a. shift your identity.

ASK CONSCIOUS QUESTIONS

*The depth of your questions dictates the depth
of your relationships.*

I n my twenties, I'd often nod and pretend I was listening to someone to disguise the fact that I was secretly thinking about a smart question I could ask. Sometimes, I'd ask questions in conversations that looked great on paper, yet sounded contrived in reality. On occasion, I found myself asking questions designed to tee up a conversation around a topic that made me feel knowledgeable and significant. Does any of the above resonate?

The truth is my younger self did the best he could with the awareness he had. For that, I'm forever thankful. Today, I realize that the depth of your relationship with yourself is positively correlated with the depth of your relationship with others. The bridge between the two is asking conscious questions. In Habit 1, you focused on building a better relationship with yourself by transforming your internal story through a series of potent questions. Now you're ready to discover how to ask conscious questions that build meaningful relationships with others.

Conscious questions are rooted in positive intentionality. Here's how I see it. Asking questions without (positive) intention leads to a conversation that lacks depth, causing an absence of intimacy in that relationship. Where there's an absence of intimacy, there's a shortage of connection, and without connection, we don't have the first building block of trust. Without trust, there is zero chance of earning relationship currency. It's as simple as that.

It goes without saying that if your questions are deficient of integrity, you're likely lacking positive intent and seeking an abundant outcome for yourself at the expense of somebody else. For example, asking a question with the intention of exploiting somebody is different than asking a question with the aim of understanding somebody. In this habit, you'll learn how to practice asking three different types of conscious questions: Storyworthy, Empathetic, and Collaborative. What do each of these question styles have in common? They are filled with (positive) intentionality and are thus conscious. Nonetheless, as you'll soon learn, conscious questions may unlock connection, but to grow it, deep listening is vital.

Through my lens, deep listening involves being truly present, detaching from your desires, and absorbing somebody's verbal and non-verbal cues, without judgement, distraction, or self-interest. You may have heard of "active listening" before, a concept introduced by Carl Rogers and Richard Farson back in 1957.[17] They presented the tool as one that "requires that we get inside the speaker, that we grasp, from his point of view, just what it is he is communicating to us. More than that, we must convey to the speaker that we are seeing things from his point of view."

Rogers and Farson believed that those who are on the receiving end of this method cultivate emotional maturity, become less defensive, and develop better self-awareness. In my opinion, active listening has its merits, but it can lead to listening to respond, being clouded by personal bias, focusing on the intellectual versus the intuitive, and simply paraphrasing what the speaker has said in the hope it makes them feel understood. Nonetheless, it is the perfect entry-point for growing in your competence as an effective listener (more on how to do this in Habit 3), so don't feel bad if active listening is the skill you lean on right now. In the meantime, let's return our focus to embracing what we call "deep listening."[18]

What's the difference between active and deep listening? Quite simply, with the former, we are focused on listening to the speaker. With the latter, we go beyond listening to the spoken word, as it requires us to go within and also listen to ourselves so we can receive energetic signals and decode the speaker's emotional state by tapping into our intuition.

Here's a brief example. Imagine you're feeling the symptoms of burnout, and your teammate is trying to help you find a solution. A teammate who's an active listener may respond by saying, "I hear you; it sounds like burnout is the problem, and you're worried about not hitting your professional goals." They heard the words coming out of your mouth. They acknowledge what you say your concern is. However, it comes across that they aren't able to fully empathize with your personal experience.

A teammate who embodies deep listening may respond by saying, "I can feel the exhaustion from your energy, and I know everything feels heavy for you right now. It seems like your mind is telling you to keep pushing through as you have professional goals you need to hit. However, your body is telling you to press pause. Given you're not used to slowing down, taking time off will be a difficult decision for you to make, even though it sounds as though that's the decision you're leaning toward." Do you see the difference? In this case, they're able to empathize with what you're experiencing, describe the energy they're receiving, and tap into their own intuition without being prescriptive.

Those last three words are extremely important for building meaningful relationships that matter. As you'll learn in the practice of asking Collaborative Questions, simply giving unsolicited advice without understanding somebody's language of service is a recipe for disaster. Ultimately, through my lens, while deep listening is our North Star, active listening is better than no listening, or mindless talking.

If you struggle with feeling reactive in conversations, being present and deeply listening, allow me to introduce you to a daily spiritual practice called "sadhana." According to Sadhguru's Isha Foundation,[19] sadhana is simply a method designed to provide a level of conscious maturity, where the need to constantly be somewhere vanishes. The concept of engaging in a daily sadhana is to transform your state into one where you can simply be in the present moment without being pulled away from the now. As I see it, the purpose is to transcend your ego, connect with your higher self, and allow inner peace to find you. The question is: How?

The beauty of it is you get to choose the modality you pursue it through—prayer, journaling, reading, meditation, yoga, exercise, breathwork—you decide! Anything practiced consistently, consciously, and with the intention of spiritual growth can be considered a sadhana.[20]

What does this mean to you in the context of our discussion? Without being dogmatic and restrictive about what is truly considered a sadhana, I invite you to think about the concept like this. With intention, craft your very own daily personal practice to put your mind, body, and spirit in alignment so you can detach yourself from your desires and have meaningful conversations throughout your day. From my own experience, not only will this help you experience more presence, but it will allow you to ask conscious questions and deeply listen with less effort. Your practice can be as simple or as complex as you like; however, the key lies in consistency. Here's an example of what this could look like.

At the start of your day, simply take a few minutes (or more) to find solitude and regulate your nervous system through one modality (or more) that energizes you the most. This feeling will inspire consistency and ensure you show up with purpose. This energy might come from the discipline itself or the feeling you receive afterward. For me, a cold plunge followed by gratitude and/or breathwork helps me activate the parasympathetic nervous system, feel a sense of calm, and remove any desperation attached to my desires. Plus, with two young children, a business, and more, I strive for progress over perfection. When I'm feeling instant gratification rear its ugly head or a lack of clarity or reactiveness, I always know my sadhana will anchor me. When you do this, you'll develop a level of trust that everything in every interaction throughout your day is happening for you and not to you. This is when presence will find you. During your daily conversations, if you observe yourself drifting, try the following mantra to trigger a mental reset: "I am here, I am present."

Don't have time to create your own daily sadhana? You either make time today, or you'll have to make the time tomorrow, once your inability to have meaningful conversations (with yourself and others) bites you in the butt. Both are hard. Simply choose your hard.

Do both of these right—ask conscious questions *and* deeply listen—and you'll begin having meaningful conversations that spark intimacy, forge trust, and develop the connective tissue required to form a lifelong bond. It's important to realize this is the path less taken. Most people are operating on autopilot, running from meeting to meeting, and stuck making a myriad of mistakes that keep them from asking conscious questions that build trust. While mistakes are necessary for reflection and growth, allow me to help you collapse the time on that journey by learning from the mistakes of others.

FOUR COMMON KILLERS OF ASKING CONSCIOUS QUESTIONS

Over the years, I've been hired by sales and customer success teams at billion-dollar organizations, purpose-driven leaders at high-growth companies, and entrepreneurs building mission-driven movements. Each of these experiences has given me a rare insight into how people communicate across different industries, roles, and parts of the world. But more importantly, it's helped me uncover the mistakes preventing people from asking conscious questions that foster meaningful conversations.

As we already know, the villain in our story is instant gratification. But let's be real for a second. Reactive behavior, the need for instant success and transactional conversations aren't a new phenomenon; they've been hardwired into us since we were children. Social Learning Theory (SLT), proposed by Albert Bandura, suggests that people learn new behaviors by observing and imitating others.[21] To grossly oversimplify this idea, SLT states that when we observe the consequences of other people's behavior, we are more likely to imitate the actions that are positively rewarded and avoid those that are punished. In turn, this leads to an acquisition of knowledge, attitudes, and belief systems.

Here's an example to illustrate this point. Back in the day, I very rarely saw kids in my class at school (or myself) being rewarded for asking curious, conscious, and interesting questions. In fact, when this did happen, we were "punished." We were met with frustration and were perceived as "unintelligent" by our classmates. What I did see was praise, acknowledgement, and rewards for those who had the right answers to questions. Through this observation, little Ravi avoided asking "stupid questions," focused on trying to be right, and shied away from being inquisitive. This habit stuck with me for years. Can you relate?

If all you've been told is that getting to the destination (the right answer) is more important than the journey (asking conscious questions), then imagine how this has impacted your everyday conversations, in business and life.

When it comes to uncovering the common pitfalls that have prevented my clients from asking conscious questions, keeping them stuck in surface level conversations, the list is endless. For brevity, I've whittled it down to my favorite four, many of which are "learned behaviors" and have been subconsciously imitated from an early age. Here's the beautiful thing: you are both the problem and the solution. This means that you (and nobody else) have the power to stop sabotaging your desires. Park your ego, get curious, and see if any of these resonate.

Conversation domination

Two words: talk time. If you're dominating a conversation using the spoken word and the amount of time you're talking is more than the person opposite you, this can be detrimental. This statement requires further nuance. However, at a fundamental level, if you're using precious time to push your agenda, solution, or viewpoint down somebody's throat without solicitation, you're talking *at them*, not *with them*.

This is grossly missing the point.

Remember, your goal is to build a trusted relationship. One way to do that is by asking conscious questions that stimulate thought, unlock new thinking, and shift perspectives. Do this right and when you do speak, your words will be potent and resonate, and you'll show them that you truly see, hear, and understand them. More on this shortly.

Trying to be interesting vs. interested

Dale Carnegie once said something along the lines of, "To be interesting, be interested."[22] Here's how I see it: in any given conversation, meeting, or presentation, your job isn't to make yourself look significant; it's to make the other person feel significant. There's a difference. (And we'll be diving deep into this in Habit 3: Unearth Your Charisma.)

Case in point. It's late 2016. I'm about to go into a critical meeting, and I arrive ten minutes early. And so does Callum.

Callum was the man of the hour. He was an advisor to the startup I was working for at the time, and he was here to gift us with his perspective on our latest product and commercial update.

"Hey, Callum, my name's Ravi. Nice to meet you!" I said with a smile and a handshake firm enough for even a president to be proud of.

I can't lie, I wanted to make a good first impression. I'd been told that Callum was a visionary, an innovator, a mover, and a shaker. I mean, can you blame my inner people-pleaser for wanting to impress?

As we sat down engaging in small talk before the rest of my team arrived, I'll never forget how the next nine minutes of that conversation went. Callum proceeded to list his accolades, awards, and career milestones like he was a waiter reciting the specials for dinner at a restaurant. I was in shock. Was Callum trying to impress ME instead?!

As Callum focused on trying to be *interesting*, he spent little to no time being *interested*. No conscious questions, no deep listening, and zero desire to learn about the human being opposite him. In almost an instant (or nine minutes, rather) Callum diminished his influence.

The result? A superficial conversation that forever left a bad taste in my mouth.

When you spend so much time trying to look interesting to others, you forget that the goal is to be interested in them using the power of conscious questions. Often, first impressions are the last ones. Consider the story you might be telling others when you're aiming to be interesting rather than interested.

Being attached to an outcome

A job interview, a sales call, a meeting with leadership—the list goes on. Enter any of these conversations attached to a specific result and you'll instantly engage in inauthentic behavior in an engineered scenario. Your body language, tone, rate of speech, energy, and more will unconsciously map to your need for an outcome within a specific timeline. This leads to behaviors that erode trust and reduce your desirability.

For example, let's say you're a salesperson who is one deal away from hitting your quota. Everything depends on the next sales call with your prospect, Amy. Instead of asking her conscious questions and deeply listening, you rush to explain the features and functionality of your solution. Instead of uncovering Amy's million-dollar problem, you rush to explain the pricing of your services. And instead of understanding if there's true alignment, you rush to offer a time-contingent discount to accelerate her buying decision. The result? Losing the deal. And more importantly, losing the relationship . . . for *life*. Little did you know, Amy just needed a little bit of TLC and a trusted guide (more on that in Habit 5) by her side to put your entire year's quota to bed. Our villain of instant gratification rears its ugly head once again.

If you ever find yourself engaging in reactive behavior like this, pause and ask yourself this: "If I were overflowing with abundance in every area of my life, how would I behave in this moment?" Once you remove your attachment to an outcome and how you believe it should unfold, you create the mental capacity for asking conscious questions that allow you to truly communicate with influence. As a result, abundance and miraculous outcomes will find you, but not always in the time or path you desire.

Asking superficial questions

In my experience, the height of emotional intimacy is when two human beings feel safe enough to exchange vulnerable stories, perspectives, and beliefs without fear of judgment. This is where true connection lies. Those who grasp this know that asking conscious questions is a beautiful path toward having a collaborative two-way conversation.

The key word here is conscious. Remember this: the depth of your questions dictates the depth of your relationships. So, asking questions just for the sake of it, asking questions that map towards a hidden agenda, and asking questions that lack genuine curiosity without care for the answer—these are behaviors that lack positive intentionality and devalue relationship currency. Transactional behavior creates surface-level relationships that are a dime a dozen.

For example, as you'll learn later in this chapter, questions like "How are you?" are lazy, mindless, and meaningless (unless used in the appropriate context). Soon we'll cover my What, Feel, Who Method where I'll teach you a simple way to ask Empathetic Questions without being fake.

THE THREE TYPES OF CONSCIOUS QUESTIONS

Now that you know what *not* to do, it's time to switch gears to the true intention of this chapter—learning to ask conscious questions that increase the depth, intimacy, and trust within any business relationship. While there are several paths at your disposal, I want to ensure you don't get diagnosed with "infobesity" (consuming high volumes of information, experiencing mental exhaustion and analysis paralysis, leaving little room for implementation) after reading this chapter. Remember, unlocking your limitless influence requires imperfect action. That's exactly why I'm going to focus on just three types of conscious questions for you to practice and implement: Storyworthy Questions that stimulate thought, Empathetic Questions that create intimacy, and Collaborative Questions that truly serve the human being opposite you. As mentioned earlier, your success with this habit lies in your ability to consistently engage in two behaviors: asking conscious questions and deeply listening, because they are two sides of the same coin.

PRACTICE: ASK STORYWORTHY QUESTIONS—
USE THEM TO STIMULATE THOUGHT AND EXTRACT A STORY

Allow me to introduce you to the power of "Storyworthy Questions" (otherwise known as open-ended questions). When you ask a Storyworthy Question, you allow somebody to travel back in time, unearth a story, and share it with you. Or even better, you receive nothing but silence, which tells somebody a story of intention about you (more on this shortly). The outcome is a transformational conversation. These are the types of questions that cannot be answered with a limited or one-word response.

For example, let's say you're speaking with a prospect who sounds like they are sick of their current supplier. Early on in the conversation, you say, "Jamie, do you want to switch suppliers?" This type of question will result in a yes, no, or maybe, stunting the rapport building journey (more on this in a second).

Alternatively, you could ask, "Jamie, can you tell me about the moment you first sensed trouble with your supplier?" When somebody has to adopt a creative mindset and tap into their imagination to answer a question they're rarely asked, beautiful things happen. Plus, when a Storyworthy Question is asked with an upward inflection, you will convey curiosity and increase your chances of building rapport.

On the other hand, we have "Factworthy Questions" (otherwise known as closed-ended questions), which often yield a yes or no response, or a reply that's confined to a finite set of answer choices. These types of questions can be incredible for gathering insightful data or factual information that provides clarity within a conversation. Factworthy Questions aren't good or bad, they must simply be used in the right context.

For example, asking your prospect the following questions would be considerably more effective than a Storyworthy Question: "Is jamie@companyxyz.com the best email address for sending you a calendar invite for our next call?" Or "Which is more important to you, the upfront integration fee or the cost of the monthly payments?" As you can see, these questions are designed to provide concise and focused responses that provide clarity for moving a conversation forward.

Nonetheless, in this habit, due to their nature, we're leaning on Storyworthy Questions to be your ticket to unlocking connection. In light of that, to ensure you ask meaningful ones, here are five key principles:

1. Ensure your questions aren't biased toward a self-serving outcome.
2. Be clear, specific, and short to avoid confusion.
3. Ask one, and only one, question to reduce decision fatigue.
4. Use upward inflection at the end of the sentence to convey curiosity and ensure your words are perceived as a question rather than a statement.
5. Start your question with phrases such as "What," "Can you tell me about," "When," "How," or "Imagine if ..." as a guideline to ensure you aren't asking Factworthy Questions.

Here are some examples of Storyworthy Questions to witness these principles in practice:

1. **What** are you personally working on right now that you're really excited about?
2. **Can you tell me about** the moment you first realized you wanted to step into a leadership role?
3. **When** did you first get the itch to start your own company?

4. If we fast forward six months from now, **how** will
you know when success has been achieved with our
partnership?

5. **Imagine if** time and resources weren't an issue, how
would this change the customer retention strategy
you've just laid out?

Ultimately, the mark of a successful Storyworthy Question is not
when somebody shares a story with you. It's not even when they go
beyond a one-word, two-word, or limited answer. It's when they say
nothing. It's when there's a brief moment of silence. And it's when
they break that silence with a vulnerable admission. Something along
the lines of, "Mmm . . . I've never been asked that before." This is
the holy grail. The true North Star of a Storyworthy Question is
stopping somebody in their tracks and provoking deep thought. Do
this right and you'll build a connection, signal a character of curiosity,
and subtly display competence without shoving it down somebody's
throat. Not only will this tell somebody a positive story about you,
but it will ensure the Three C's begin working their magic.

Uncovering emotional levers

An emotional lever is a moment (or series of moments) in a conversation that displays high levels of emotional charge (positive and negative). Storyworthy Questions reveal these levers. Deep listening
enables you to decode what each lever means. Returning to our prior
example: you asked, "Jamie, can you tell me about the moment you
first sensed trouble with your supplier?" If you do extract a story as
a response, sit back, listen to understand, and identify an emotional
lever that'll increase the depth of the conversation.

To uncover emotional levers, the key lies in observing a deviation in one's baseline behavior in the following categories:

1. Verbal communication
2. Nonverbal communication
3. Energy

When identified and decoded, this allows you to formulate a question that effectively pulls this lever and progresses the conversation around a theme the person you're speaking to deeply cares about. For example, let's say Jamie ends their response to your question with "... and I was so unhappy when we received no warning of a *price increase!*" As they share this, you notice the following:

- The volume of their voice spikes.
- Their tone sounds angry and their energy shifts.
- They emphasize the words "price increase".
- They increase their rate of speech.
- They fold their arms and their body language becomes closed.

As you can see, in just fourteen words, you've uncovered a series of behaviors that are starkly different from Jamie's baseline behavior (which you observed at the start of your conversation) within our three categories. It's official. Through conscious questioning and deep listening, you have uncovered an emotional lever. This is a good thing. Not only does Jamie feel safe enough to have this conversation with you, but you now have earned the opportunity to increase the depth of your connection. Let's discuss three examples of where you could take the conversation next.

Example one: mirroring. This is a communication strategy, popularized by former FBI negotiator Chris Voss,[23] in which a person repeats specific words, phrases, or parts of what somebody says, or mimics the nonverbal communication of the other party to elicit trust. In the context of the former, you would repeat the last one to three words of what Jamie said (word for word), using an upward inflection to ensure it sounds like a curious question.

For example, "A price increase?" All of a sudden, Jamie continues with, "Yes, you won't believe what they did. Last month they hit us with an 18 percent . . . " And just like that, you're receiving more granularity and digging deeper into the heart of why he wants to leave his current supplier: a lack of trust.

Example two: showcase deep listening in combination with a follow-up Storyworthy Question. For example, "I sense that you're feeling frustrated, and I know this must be difficult for you since you have a personal relationship with the CEO of your supplier. Given the lack of a warning around the price increase, it seems like the trust has been broken in your relationship. Knowing what you know now, what is of most importance to you when choosing your next supplier?" In this example, you're not just able to understand Jamie's point of view and repeat the language they used to describe their challenge, but you're also able to illuminate what's not being said (with warmth), and ask a Storyworthy Question that stimulates thought.

Example three: my What, Feel, Who Method. Think about it like this: **What** does Jamie care about? An unexpected price increase. How do they **feel** about it? Unhappy. **Who** in their life is this impacting? Themselves. When you tune in to such intricacies, it allows for a follow-up conscious question, such as, "What was it specifically about the unexpected price increase that made you unhappy?" This is the short-form version of my What, Feel, Who Method. I will dive deeper into this in the next practice, but for now, just remember that the depth of your questions dictates the depth of your relationships.

Uncovering emotional levers is a true skill, and it requires you to be truly present with another human being. The truth is, giving somebody your undivided attention is a gift in today's distraction-filled world. If you're thinking about your desires, your to-do list, or anything else that's competing for your attention at that given moment, you are doing the person in front of you a disservice. Plus, this is a slippery slope to taking the path of least resistance and resorting to unintended reactive behavior. This is just one reason why having a daily sadhana can shift the trajectory of your life— you can increase your presence, reduce the volume on your needs, and deeply listen to your conversation partner without expectation or bias.

Remember, Storyworthy Questions are beautiful conversation starters. Combine this with deep listening and impactful follow-up questions and you'll begin to develop better relationships, not just in business, but in every walk of life. However, if you want to build trusted relationships that last, the key lies in showing (not telling) somebody that you care about, what they care about.

PRACTICE: ASK EMPATHETIC QUESTIONS—
THE WHAT, FEEL, WHO METHOD FOR CREATING INTIMACY
Have you ever heard of "Sawubona"? This is a Zulu greeting that means "I see you." The idea is to recognize the value and dignity of each and every human you come into contact with, accepting their humanity in its entirety and giving them your undivided

presence. One common response to this greeting is "Shiboka," which means "I exist for you."[24] Beautiful, huh?

Now, take a brief moment to picture your everyday greeting with the people you meet. In comparison, doesn't yours feel rushed, unconscious, and devoid of empathy? Empathy is an energy that, once transferred, shows somebody you are deeply interested in what they are emotionally invested in. So, how can we show somebody we care, without telling them we care, and signal genuine interest without being fake?

Let's dig deeper and uncover the full framework of my What, Feel, Who Method. This simple process was born out of my own frustration with being on the receiving end of superficial greetings and questions that led to a deterioration of trust in certain relationships in my life. Today, I'm going to share it with you to ensure you don't enforce such an experience on others.

First, picture this. You're about to step into your initial 1:1 meeting with Zander, a new recruit on your team. He's your first meeting of the day, you've had a sip of coffee, and you've got the mental capacity to be truly present. As you want to put your best foot forward, you ask a series of impactful questions during the conversation. "Zander, what are you working on outside of work that's really important to you right now?" "How do you feel about it?" "Who in your life is this impacting the most?" These three simple, conscious questions (asked separately and intentionally) will unearth **what** is important to Zander in this season of his personal life, how he **feels** about it, and **who** it is impacting. A meaningful conversation ensues and a connection is formed. Now, the question is, what do you do with this information?

The key lies in following up your initial series of questions with an Empathetic Question that displays care. This looks like showing (not just telling) him that you are interested in the very thing he's emotionally invested in. When used with integrity, not only will you build trust and loyalty, but you'll become the type of leader others want to follow. (More on this idea in the Conclusion: Be a Symbol.)

Fast forward to two weeks later, and there you are, walking into your follow-up meeting with Zander. Except this time it's a different story. You're feeling reactive, distracted (it sounds like you skipped your daily sadhana!), and your day is filled with back-to-back meetings. As a result, you rush into your office, remove your jacket, haphazardly put down your phone, and ask in a flustered manner, "Hey, Zander, how are you?" before taking a bite of your sandwich. One word: lazy. In a relationship where you're seeking depth, this question is anything but conscious. But what should you have done differently?

In your initial meeting with Zander, your series of questions was designed to uncover the What, Feel, and Who. The key lies in asking an Empathetic Question in your next meeting, incorporating the very information you learned prior:

- **What** is important to them?
- How do they **feel** about it?
- And **who** is this impacting?

For example, in your follow-up meeting you could say, "Zander, the last time we spoke, you mentioned you were moving home [WHAT] and that you were feeling stressed [FEEL] because your daughter [WHO] was unhappy about the change. How has she settled into her new environment?"

Can you see the difference between this question and a casual, "How are you?" Caring about what Zander cares about, using his own language to describe how he felt, and displaying genuine interest in where he's at with his personal challenge is something that's missing when you're too busy focused on your own challenges, desires, and agenda.

By asking an Empathetic Question using this method, you give people the stage to share what's deeply important to them and spark intimacy, all while creating a layer of psychological safety in the relationship. Whether you're communicating with a prospect, an existing customer, a partner, an investor, or a teammate, this method will ensure you build trusted relationships, both in business and in life.

As you'll notice, if you didn't uncover the What, Feel, Who in your prior conversation, you'll struggle to use this method in your current conversation. This points to one thing I said at the top of this chapter: conscious questions may unlock connection, but deep listening grows it.

Remember the day after my first cold plunge when I experienced flu like symptoms? As you implement this practice in the wild and depart from your current behavior in conversations, you too may experience flu like conversational symptoms. Meaning, it will feel strange, awkward, and inauthentic at the beginning. Good. This means you're on the right track. As you work toward unconscious competence, you must normalize these feelings and even welcome them. And just like cold water immersion is now second nature to me, the same will be true for you when asking conscious questions and engaging in deep listening. I'm sure of it.

Speaking of behaviors that create an identity shift, I'm about to share another type of conscious question that I can (almost) guarantee will result in a meaningful two-way conversation. It all boils down to one thing: supporting another human being in the way they like to be supported.

PRACTICE: ASK COLLABORATIVE QUESTIONS—UNCOVER SOMEBODY'S LANGUAGE OF SERVICE

It's the summer of 2022, and my wife and I are sweating buckets as we watch one of her best friends tie the knot on a grueling hot day. My wife was also heavily pregnant with our first child. All day and all night, she was peppered with questions about motherhood, yet one of them stood out the most: "Are you going to breastfeed?"

When my wife divulged that we had made the decision to bottle-feed our newborn, she was met with a barrage of unsolicited advice from a complete stranger. As I observed their conversation from afar, I saw her receiving the "hairdryer treatment" (being reprimanded from point blank range) from this well-intentioned wedding guest. I later learned the topic in question was around why "breast is best." But in that moment, my wife wasn't seeking advice. Yet, she received it, unsolicited, in truckloads. The result? She left that conversation feeling misunderstood.

What about you? Have you ever been on the receiving end of unsolicited advice when all you wanted was for somebody to listen or ask meaningful questions? If you're nodding, did this experience leave you feeling seen, heard, and understood?

I didn't think so.

Everybody has their own unique way in which they like to be supported. The goal of this practice is to uncover somebody's language of service so you can have a collaborative conversation. You must ask yourself: Are you supporting the relationships that matter to you using your path for a resolution or theirs? Earning relationship currency requires you to communicate in the same (service) language as the person you're trying to connect with. Get this right and you'll open the doors to becoming somebody's trusted guide and achieve limitless influence (something we'll touch upon in Habit 5).

But how do we uncover somebody's language of service in a business context?

Here's the scenario: you're sitting in a quarterly business review with a client of yours, Julie. She isn't her normal self, and before you know it, your Empathetic Question using the What, Feel, Who Method reveals all. "Julie, the last time we spoke, you mentioned you were throwing your name in the hat for a promotion, and that you were feeling excited because this felt like a new chapter for you. How did things play out?" Unfortunately, Julie was passed up for a promotion, again. You feel her pain, because you were in the same position at your last company. Not only that, you're on the other side of that problem and believe you have the solution. Instead of shoving your story, experience, and advice down her throat, you engage in three simple steps:

- Step 1: Lead with empathy.
- Step 2: Label the emotion.
- Step 3: Ask a Collaborative Question.

Here's what it looks like in practice . . .

- Step 1: "Eurgh, Julie, I know how important the promotion was to you."
- Step 2: "It sounds like you're feeling disheartened."
- Step 3: "How can I support you best here? Would you like me to simply listen, give you my perspective, or ask you questions that'll help you find a solution?"

You may have noticed something interesting. Inside step one, we use empathy to show that we are interested in what Julie is emotionally invested in (the desired promotion), making her feel heard. Inside step two, we use "labeling." In this context (versus what you observed in Habit 1), labeling is a communication strategy in which you highlight and verbalize specific emotions or feelings that are visible but have not been directly expressed using the spoken word.[25] Furthermore, by beginning with phrases such as "It sounds like," "It feels like," or "It seems as though" you avoid being prescriptive if you're not fully certain about the emotional energy you're receiving. This is followed by inserting Julie's overarching sentiment in this case, "disheartened", creating a feeling of mutual understanding, and making her feel seen.

Finally, by providing optionality with your Collaborative Question in the final step, you make Julie feel understood. However, if all else fails in the moment, and you go blank, ensure the one thing you nail is step three, where you ask a Collaborative Question that allows you to uncover her language of service and how she likes to be supported by others.

In light of that, here's the exact script once again: "How can I support you best here? Would you like me to simply listen, give you my perspective, or ask you questions that'll help you find a solution?"

In my own life, the people I trust are the ones who deeply listen and ask conscious questions. A combination of these two paths is my language of service. However, if I assume that we all thrive using the same support system, my communication will be narrow, ignorant, and misinformed, leaving my conversation partner feeling misunderstood. Remember, our job is to serve the human being we're trying to connect with.

To ensure you don't drown in the deep end, here are three tips for execution:

1. Display a warm tone and ensure your North Star is nothing other than sitting with them in their emotional state without judgment.
2. If there's silence after your question, don't fill it. Give the other person the space to digest and respond.
3. If they reply to your collaborative question with, "I don't know," lead with a conscious question. The key lies in uncovering clues as to whether they are a verbal processor who needs the space to talk, somebody who needs perspective from a trusted guide, or an individual who's looking to unlock a creative solution by being asked thoughtful questions.

As stated, when you began your journey inside this book, there are no trophies on offer for anything other than imperfect action. So, how can you implement what you've learned in this habit? Whether you're speaking to a prospect, partner, existing customer, or team member, developing a "Conscious Question Closet" with the three different types of conscious questions you've learned will help you get the ball rolling as you climb the conscious competence ladder with this skill.

If you need a Quickstart Guide to start building your Conscious Question Closet, I've got that queued up on the book's free resource page available to you over at theravirajani.com/bookresources.

I've said it before and I'll say it again: conscious questions may unlock connection, but deep listening grows it. As you can see, you can't have one without the other, my friend. Whether it's asking Storyworthy Questions, Empathetic Questions, or Collaborative Questions, your ability to deeply listen to another human being can mean the difference between being forgettable and unforgettable.

Our next step is redefining charisma, unearthing it within yourself, and using it to make somebody feel significant in your presence. Everything you learned in this habit supports what you're about to learn in the next. There is a method to this madness. Let's get into it!

THE HIGHLIGHT REEL

- The depth of your relationship with yourself is positively correlated with the depth of your relationship with others. The bridge between the two is asking conscious questions.
- Deep listening goes beyond absorbing the spoken word alone. It requires you to embrace presence, detach from your desires, and uncover somebody's verbal and nonverbal cues, while recruiting your intuition throughout the experience.
- The true North Star of a Storyworthy Question is stopping somebody in their tracks, provoking deep thought, and stimulating silence.
- To uncover emotional levers, the key lies in observing a deviation in one's baseline behavior within the following categories: verbal communication, nonverbal communication, and energy.
- If you didn't uncover the What, Feel, and Who in your prior conversation, you'll struggle to ask a follow-up Empathetic Question in your current conversation.

- Ask a Collaborative Question to decipher somebody's language of service to ensure you're supporting them in a way they'd like to be supported.

UNEARTH YOUR CHARISMA

*True charisma makes others feel significant
in your presence.*

Growing up, I had charisma all wrong. I thought it was about showcasing what one would label "extroverted" character traits and receiving attention, accolades, and awards. But true charisma isn't about making yourself look significant; it's about making others feel significant in your presence. When somebody feels like they matter when they're around you, a relationship built on trust is an organic byproduct.

In the world we live in today, charisma, by definition, is viewed as a personality trait reserved for a select few. According to the *Cambridge Dictionary*, charisma is defined as "a specific quality that some people have naturally that makes them able to influence other people and attract their attention and admiration."[26] I don't subscribe to the "some people" or "attention and admiration" parts of this definition. Culturally, we seem to believe that charisma is reserved for Hollywood actors, musicians, and leaders of iconic movements. But as we've already touched upon, recognition is not the signifier of charisma. I define charisma as an innate superpower, which everybody possesses, that helps others feel significant in your presence, increasing your capacity for influence. You don't *become* charismatic, because you were already *born* charismatic.

When I think of somebody who authentically embodies this definition, I think of a man by the name of RJ Silva. RJ had more personality, confidence, and flair than I'd ever seen in a human being before. Back in my twenties, before I landed a full-time role on RJ's wider team in the world of investment banking, I started as a green summer intern trying to get his seal of approval.

Every single day, I would quietly observe him from afar. From the moment RJ stepped into the office, somebody wanted something from him. His time, energy, and resources were consistently in high demand, yet three things always blew me away about him. Every single time he saw me, he delivered a one-liner that would have me in stitches. Every single time he greeted me, his warm eye contact and genuine smile made me feel like he deeply cared. And every single time I had the opportunity to steal a moment of his precious time, he never made me feel less than due to my lack of seniority. He treated every person exactly the same, regardless of who they were, their role, or title.

Every single interaction with RJ left me better off than when he found me. I'll never forget the time he took me out for lunch and peppered me with conscious questions, shared stories that were magnetizing, and empowered me to own my genius from day one. When I was around RJ, it felt safe to remove my mask and be who I truly was. He oozed charisma and was the type of leader that I (and others) wanted to follow.

Every human being is born with this innate superpower. For some, their comfort with silence and ability to create the space for a meaningful conversation may be their vehicle for charisma. For others, it could be their ability to share vulnerable stories that give people permission to be themselves. You get the picture, right? As you embody this habit, don't forget, we all have a unique genius, and thus, charisma looks different on different people. This habit is designed to redefine how you see charisma and help you unearth it for yourself through communicating with influence.

Once you embody true charisma, not only will you have more influence and become a symbol (more on this in Conclusion: Be a Symbol) for those around you like RJ did, but you'll develop a magnetic aura that'll pull the right people, opportunities, and circumstances into your world. So, how does one unearth their charisma? Alongside the practices divulged in this habit, it requires commitment to a journey of introspection so you can become deeply comfortable in your own skin. This is something you implicitly agreed to do after deciding to tame your cravings for instant gratification (in the Introduction) and dedicate yourself to an adventure of internal growth (in Habit 1). Do this right and watch the magic unfold:

- Team members will drop their pretense, stop posturing, and won't feel the need to be somebody they're not when they're around you because they feel safe enough to be themselves.
- Direct reports will feel inspired to own their imperfections and leverage their unique genius to create more abundance for themselves, the company, and you.
- Customers will be open to change and see you as a trusted guide they can rely on.

- Business partners will experience little to no anxiety about sharing their differences in perspectives, beliefs, and viewpoints, fostering a collaborative culture.
- Prospects will feel comfortable enough to say "no" to you so you can get to the heart of their truth without being ghosted.

As such, the name of the game through Habit 3 is simple: learning how to communicate in a way that makes others feel like they matter in your presence, which includes the three keys of understanding, owning your imperfections so you can become more influential, and giving (and receiving) authentic compliments that make others feel seen. Without further wait, let's get into it.

MAKING PEOPLE FEEL UNDERSTOOD

I've witnessed relationships disintegrate into dust because one party doesn't feel understood by the other in a conversation. Feeling misunderstood is what creates actual misunderstandings, and misunderstandings deteriorate trust.

In business, we use platitudes such as "I hear you," "I'm on the same page," and "I understand what you're saying." The truth is, words are cheap when one's behavior isn't congruent with the words coming out of their mouth. The one question we should ask ourselves is how can we show somebody we truly understand them without actually saying it?

PRACTICE: THE THREE KEYS OF UNDERSTANDING

In a nutshell, the three keys will help you make somebody feel understood in a way that they've never experienced before. Its effectiveness will increase with your level of competence. However, this isn't a magic formula; see this as a set of keys that can unlock trusted relationships when infused with your own unique voice, expertise, and personality.

Key 1: Reduce internal noise

As we discussed in Habit 2, actually listening to another human being is essential to the depth of your relationships. More than a skill, it's a lifestyle. A prerequisite for that is being fully present, drowning out external distractions, and learning how to reduce the volume of your internal noise. Let's revisit one important tool to help you do exactly that and introduce a new one into the mix.

If you haven't already, remember to create your own daily sadhana. This will help you detach from your desires, be in the now, and give the person opposite you the gift of presence. Whatever modality you choose, focus on consistency, purpose, and progress over perfection every single day. Throughout your daily interactions, if you observe yourself drifting from any conversation at any moment, silently do an internal reset and say to yourself: *I am here, I am present.*

Now, let's introduce a new tool into the mix. Have you ever heard of the physiological sigh? It's a technique that was discovered in the 1930s to help us rapidly regain control from feelings of stress or anxiety. I first stumbled upon this tool through Stanford Neuroscientist, Dr. Andrew Huberman.[27] To do the physiological sigh, take two deep inhales through your nose and one long exhale through your mouth with pursed lips. Almost instantly, you'll experience more calm, less tension, and a sense of presence. Repeat it a few times if you need another hit of the good stuff.

Key 2: Reveal their desired reality
Picture this, you're now in the thick of a conversation accompanied by physical and mental presence. The goal is simple: to unlock insights and uncover your conversation partner's desired reality. This is done by asking Storyworthy Questions, identifying emotional levers, and posing Empathatic and Collaborative Questions.

Specifically, your goal is to unearth the answers to the following six questions:

1. What do they desire?
2. What does life look like (personally and professionally) when they reach the promised land?
3. What obstacle is getting in their way?
4. What path have they already tried that hasn't worked?
5. How do they feel about their status quo?
6. What does life look like in a year's time if nothing changes?

Even if you are using AI to record and summarize your calls, I invite you to keep it old school. Take out a pen and notepad and take physical notes. Write down things such as:

- Topics in the conversation that receive a higher talk time and specific words that are emphasized.
- Inconsistencies between their desires and current behavior.
- Shifts in their speech: pitch, pace, tone, volume, or intonation.

- Moments of silence, or questions that result in pacifying behavior to soothe their internal discomfort. For example, deflecting or touching one's face.
- Words, phrases, and statements they use to describe their current and future states (e.g., if a leader says they want to overcome a "disengaged workplace," then write those exact words down instead of scribbling your own phrase to describe your perception of their reality).

As you initially embody this process, you may sound scripted, feel inauthentic, or struggle to get the answers to the above six questions in a sequential and logical order (if at all). Traditionally, when this occurs, it's a signal of two things: you're either engaging in a box-ticking exercise and are viewing this as a magic formula, or you're simply trying something new that will take time to feel instinctive and unconscious.

For example, let's say mid-conversation you ask the following question, "What would need to happen over the next twelve months for you to feel that you and your team had a successful year—and why?" This is a conscious question (more specifically, a Storyworthy Question) to unlock the answer to question 1: What does somebody desire in this season of their life? Hopeful and excited to see the magic unfold, you receive a disheartening (and awkward) silence. You're tempted to break the silence (to soothe your discomfort) and swiftly move on to the next question in fear of not being able to fully extract somebody's desired reality. In that moment there are several ways to respond instead. For example, sitting with somebody in their silence, honoring the pause, and allowing them to share their thoughts without expectation of how you want the conversation to look. Since this creates the space for a meaningful conversation, you now have several tools at your disposal; for example, asking a follow-up Storyworthy Question, a Collaborative Question, or simply honoring the nonlinear process and meeting your conversation partner where they're at without judgement. Context is king. And if you noticed, your question did exactly what it was supposed to: provoke deep thought. As we discussed in Habit 2, this is the holy grail of a Storyworthy Question. Over time, you'll find yourself feeling comfortable with uncomfortable silence and other unexpected scenarios that come your way. As you move toward a world of unconscious competence with this practice, don't be afraid to inject your expertise and intuition into the framework laid out (or to eventually break it and create your own).

Key 3: Communicate for understanding

Once you have unearthed all the relevant information required to gain an understanding of their truth, the goal is to hit pause on the conversation, in real time, and hit them with a sixty-second movie trailer of their desired reality. The idea is to paint a vivid picture of where they are today, where they want to be, and who or what the villain is that is preventing them from reaching the promised land (from their lens and perception). You want to show them you truly understand them without having to spell it out to them. Not only will this progress the conversation, but it will make them more receptive to change. At the end, you'll ask the following question to seek clarification on whether you've hit the nail on the head or delivered a dud: "Is there anything I've missed or misunderstood?" More on this in just a moment. For now, let's dig deeper and see what this looks like in practice.

Here's an example template you can adapt for any conversation with a prospect, customer, employee, team member, vendor—you name it. You can also access this in the book's free resources page over at theravirajani.com/bookresources.

It sounds like you're looking to [insert the answer to question 1], as it will help you [insert the answer to question 2], but what's getting in the way is [insert the answer to question 3].

And even though you've tried [insert the answer to question 4], something still seems off, leaving you feeling [insert the answer to question 5]. If everything stays as is, you [insert the answer to question 6]. Is there anything I've missed or misunderstood?

To use a professional example, here's a variation of how this may look when speaking to a direct report:

"It sounds like you're looking to land a promotion over the next eighteen months, as the increase in salary will help you save for buying your first home, and the extra responsibility will help you grow into a leadership role.

However, what's getting in the way is your challenge with communicating with brevity to the C-suite, and even though you've had executive communication training, something still seems off, leaving you feeling resentful.

If everything stays as is, you will feel regretful as you won't have achieved what you believe you're capable of. Is there anything I've missed or misunderstood?"

Or, when communicating with a prospect or customer:

"It sounds like you're looking to increase revenue by 19 percent over the next twelve months, as it will help the company achieve

a banner year and you personally in getting the promotion you've been gunning for!

However, what's getting in the way is that your salespeople are spending 34 percent of their time on non-revenue-generating activities, and even though you've upgraded your CRM, something still seems off, leaving you feeling stuck.

If everything stays as is, you won't be perceived as a leader internally, and you'll feel directly responsible for the weak revenue growth. Is there anything I've missed or misunderstood?"

The most important piece of this practice is ending with the question, *Is there anything I've missed or misunderstood?* It shows vulnerability. Why? Because it signals that you're open to being corrected.

This level of humility not only builds trust, but it removes the risk of creating a misunderstanding and leaving somebody feeling misunderstood. Once again, to convey deep curiosity, use an upward inflection to transform your words into a question, versus a downward inflection, which could create friction.

Traditionally, once you ask this question, one of the following three scenarios will unfold:

1. They will light up like a Christmas tree and confirm that you're spot on, stimulating a meaningful conversation.
2. They will partially agree with what you've said, but they'll also illuminate areas that require more granularity, giving you further information on what's important to them and what part of your understanding requires iteration.
3. You miss the mark, own the disconnect, and humanize yourself as you pull the conversation back to

basics while you receive feedback on what you've missed or misunderstood.

Here's the good news. Every single one of these outcomes is a "win," as they all point toward the same North Star: making somebody feel significant in your presence. When you reduce your internal noise, reveal their desired reality, and communicate for understanding, you'll treat somebody as a human being instead of a meal ticket to your desires. This will be seen as contrarian and a breath of fresh air by those who have been exposed to conversations with hidden agendas.

Now, some of you may be thinking, "This all sounds great Ravi, but if I simply repeat what I've heard from my conversation partner, won't I sound like a glorified parrot and create an instant disconnect?" As you may have noticed, our template and examples lean on active listening as our vehicle for success. Here's why: from my own experience, active listening is an easier entry point in comparison to "deep listening." Furthermore, it's extremely likely that your conversation partner has never heard their desired reality being relayed back to them in a logical sequence of events. Delivered in this manner, you repeating what you heard them say (using their language) can create a unique "aha moment" for the person opposite you, allowing them to see their problem in a way they've never seen it before. As you implement this in the wild, remember, active listening is arguably better than no listening or mindless talking. Embrace this as a new skill and give yourself the grace to grow over time . . . I know I did!

IMPERFECTION = CONNECTION
Now that we've addressed how the three keys of understanding build trust and illuminate our commitment to making somebody

feel like they matter in our presence, allow me to introduce you to another path to unearth your charisma: imperfection.

Picture this. It's the summer of 2022, and I'm on an alignment call with the COO of a SaaS company who was in search of a communication and storytelling speaker. A few minutes into our chat and I'm feeling kinda spicy. I lean forward, smile, and say, "Ahhh, that's an awesome picture of your daughters in the background there."

He pauses. In utter confusion, he turns his head around to look back at the photo I'm referring to. Pin-drop silence. His head slowly turns back around, and he's grinning like a Cheshire cat.

He bites his lip, shakes his head, and—still smiling—awkwardly says, "That person there . . . she's not my daughter . . . that's my wife!"

I. Was. Mortified.

As I'm squirming like a worm and fumbling my words like a Looney Tune, it dawns on me: *Whatever happens, Rav, this story will be one for the books!*

After a brief laugh and an instantly humanizing moment in our conversation, we continued speaking for over an hour. By the end of our meeting, I was hired. As they say, you can't say the right thing to the wrong person or the wrong thing to the right person.

Here's why I'm telling you this, my friend: imperfect moments are beautiful opportunities for connection. As motivational youth speaker Josh Shipp once said, "Your imperfections make you human and your humanity makes you influential."[28] When you "break character" you'll be seen as a relatable human being. This is where connection lies.

Don't believe me? In 2020, Trustpilot and Canvas8 partnered and conducted a survey on more than six thousand consumers across the UK, US, and France to determine how different types of online reviews accelerated or damaged trust. It turns out that one of the four major trends among those surveyed was that people trust authenticity more than perfection.

They found that 49 percent of global consumers felt that perfect reviews and ratings were seen as too good to be true. Specifically, over half of consumers (55 percent in the US and 52 percent in the UK) had more faith in reviews that were deemed imperfect, because less-than-perfect proved authenticity. Furthermore, going beyond reviews, global consumers were in search of brands that displayed authentic behavior, with 64 percent preferring to buy from a company who was responsive, compared to one that appeared faultless on the surface. Where there was imperfection, there was connection.[29]

The last time I checked, we were all still spiritual beings having a human experience. Denying your imperfection would mean denying your humanity. The next time you experience an "imperfect moment" in a meeting, pitch, or conversation, welcome it as though it's a gift in disguise. Take a deep breath, acknowledge it, and watch the magic unfold.

Speaking of the art of acknowledgement, that's exactly where we are headed next, to unearth our innate superpower of charisma.

ACKNOWLEDGING OTHERS FOR THEIR "GENIUS"

I believe everybody has a genius. Is it your natural flair for articulating complex ideas in a simple way? Is it your ability to code your way out of a paper bag? Or is it the depth of your empathy that helps you connect with people in a profound way? The list goes on. Whatever your genius, it's not only your ticket to your desires; it's your unique path to impacting the world. But when was the last time we acknowledged and celebrated one another for our genius? One way to do this is by giving genuine compliments *without* being fake. Do this right and you'll create more intimacy, inspire action, and cultivate loyalty in your relationships. This is the power of making somebody feel significant in your presence.

In my own life, when mentors, teammates, and peers recognized me for my genius and saw me for who I truly am, it made me want to run through a brick wall for them. It also inspired me to own my uniqueness and stop "dimming my light" in a society obsessed with telling us to color between the lines. But how does one give a genuine compliment that acknowledges somebody's genius without sounding superficial?

In a world of "go, go, go," it can be easy to fly through our day on autopilot and operate without intention. This leads to giving compliments that lack depth or, even worse, sound engineered due to a hidden agenda rooted in instant gratification. And even if we are present with another human being and give them the gift of our attention, it can be difficult to frame a compliment in a meaningful way, especially in a business setting.

Consider this example. You're at a conference and have just listened to Natalie Forenam, the CEO of your biggest revenue-generating client, deliver a killer keynote presentation. You enjoyed her talk so much that you walk over and offer her a compliment. This is what comes out:

"Hey, Natalie, awesome presentation!"

Full stop. That's it. A superficial compliment that lacks depth. Natalie smiles, says thank you (because she has to), and the conversation moves on to corporate niceties. In essence, your compliment lacked three things: authenticity, specificity, and impact. Allow me to introduce you to my ASI Framework.

PRACTICE: GIVING GENUINE COMPLIMENTS
USING THE ASI FRAMEWORK

In the context of this approach, the "A" stands for authenticity, meaning lead with a genuinely positive observation. "S" is for specificity, meaning quit being generic. And the "I" is for impact, where you acknowledge how this moment personally affected you.

During Natalie's keynote, she shared a vulnerable story with the audience that deeply resonated with you. It sparked an emotion, shifted your perspective, and inspired you to create change in your own life. So, what might a genuine compliment that encapsulates these sentiments and uses this framework look like?

"Hey, Natalie, that was the most impactful presentation I've heard all day. That story you shared in the first few minutes about struggling with crippling self-doubt as a new CEO was eye-opening and powerful! Your message has given me the permission to be more open with my struggles as a new leader. Thank you for that."

Can you see the difference between "awesome presentation" and the compliment above? Not only have you acknowledged Natalie for her genius of storytelling, but you've made her feel significant in your presence.

"Awesome presentation" is a throwaway comment. Not just because it's missing the ASI framework, but also because it lacks intimacy. There's no proximity between you and what you think about her presentation or the impact she's had on you by what she's shared. By using the word "I" (as in "one of the most impactful presentations *I've* ever heard) and attaching the compliment to you directly, it increases its level of warmth, shortens the connection gap, and organically creates intimacy.

According to Professor Norihiro Sadato, the study lead and professor at the National Institute for Physiological Sciences in

Japan, when we receive a compliment, it activates the same part of our brain (the striatum) that lights up when we receive a financial reward.[30] So, not only does giving a meaningful compliment make you more likeable; it makes you sticky and memorable, too. In short, do this right, and you'll become unforgettable.

Now, as you consider putting the ASI framework to use, I want you to remember not to weaponize this. In light of that, here are three things I invite you to think about: First, quality over quantity. If you don't have something truly worth saying, don't say anything at all. A fake compliment will decelerate trust. On the other hand, too many compliments will dilute trust, feel gimmicky, and create a perceived status imbalance in the conversation. Remember, we are here to *influence*, not manipulate. Second: intention. If you're only providing a compliment to butter someone up with the hope it'll bring you closer to your desires, you're sliding into the realm of reactive behavior. Not only that, people can feel the energy of somebody looking to "take" something from them by the end of the conversation. Finally, it's not just about what you say but about how you say it. You want to sound conversational, maintain eye contact, and exude warmth. Remember, you are giving somebody a verbal gift, so let's act like it.

Just like every other practice in this book, giving genuine compliments is a process that may not feel comfortable right away. (Return to the piece on the competence learning model in "Master and Embody What's in This Book" if you need a refresher on how to measure your growth with this practice.)

PRACTICE: RECEIVING COMPLIMENTS WITH GRACE

Now, of course, on the other side of giving compliments is receiving them.

Get this. Back in Boston, some years ago, a study found that 70 percent of people experienced feelings of discomfort or embarrassment when receiving a compliment.[31] I used to be terrible at receiving them. I would deflect, disassociate from the acknowledgement, and subconsciously resist them. Resonate?

Here's how I see it in this season of my life.

When somebody gives me a sincere compliment, it's a gift. If you make a joke, instantly compliment them in return, or convince them that you're not actually that great, then you're rejecting their gift. And in rejecting it, you're signaling to them that what they've said doesn't matter. This does everything but make somebody feel significant.

Here's something else to consider: resistance to being recognized for your genius might be data pointing you toward a story you're telling yourself about not being "worthy" or "enough." This is something to sit with as you go deeper into the inner work you've already committed to inside of Habit 1. I've said it before and I'll say it again: the inner work makes the dream work.

As mentioned, I used to suck at receiving compliments. Today, I focus on accepting them with grace, absorbing them with warmth, and ensuring my conversation partner feels my gratitude. Here are three simple steps I personally embody:

- Step 1: I pause for a moment to truly absorb and receive their gift.
- Step 2: I smile with genuine warmth.
- Step 3: I showcase open and positive body language (examples coming momentarily) and acknowledge their compliment with gratitude. For example, "Thank you for your kind words. I truly receive that."

Okay, so what do I mean when I say open and positive body language? I'm talking about:

- Facing the person you're communicating with
- Making direct eye contact
- Tapping into an authentic emotion of joy and engaging in a "Duchenne smile," involving the activation of the muscles around the eyes and mouth [32]
- Open hand gestures
- Upright posture

Receiving a compliment with grace not only tells somebody a story about your self-worth, but it ensures you don't reject their verbal gift or your own acceptance of the genius you've been given.

As we head to the next habit, remember: you don't *become* charismatic, because you were *born* charismatic. When you embody the three keys of understanding, embrace that imperfection equals connection, and acknowledge others for their genius (while also owning your own), you'll begin unearthing the charisma that already lives inside of you. Furthermore, by showing compassion, integrity, and respect, you'll activate the second ingredient within the Three C's of Trust: character. These are just a small number of practices to begin implementing, but don't overlook their potency in helping you build trusted relationships. Do this right and you'll never look at charisma the same way again.

So, where to next? Do you remember at the start of this book where I mentioned the phrase "wax on, wax off" from the original *Karate Kid* movie? See, Daniel was forced to paint a fence, sand the floor, and wax Mr. Miyagi's cars. Why? Secretly, Miyagi was giving him the muscle memory required to learn the principles of

Karate and defend himself when it mattered the most. Just like how my mum, Ram, and everybody in between took a leaf out of the Miyagi playbook and secretly exposed me to the art of communication, now, my friend, it's your turn. You are about to be Miyagi'd. In the next habit, you'll see how truly embodying each habit prior will help you in telling compelling stories that inspire change. Let's get into it!

THE HIGHLIGHT REEL

1. Charisma is an innate superpower that everybody possesses, which helps others feel significant in your presence, increasing your capacity for influence.
2. "Is there anything I've missed or misunderstood?" This question helps you communicate for understanding and displays vulnerability as you signal an openness to being corrected.
3. Imperfect moments are beautiful opportunities to "break character" and increase connection.
4. When you acknowledge somebody for their genius with authenticity, specificity, and impact, you'll cultivate trust, intimacy, and loyalty.
5. Don't forget, giving compliments and receiving them with grace are two sides of the same coin.

TELL STORIES THAT INSPIRE CHANGE

A social proof story is the ultimate trust accelerator.

n the summer of 2023, I delivered the keynote speech for Oracle NetSuite's US Sales Kick Off. This was a career highlight for me. Over 2,500 sales and account management professionals gathered to learn how to craft a story that would allow them to inspire change among their prospects and customers. The story in question? It's what I now call the "Social Proof Story." I'm talking about a narrative that unfolds in a sequential series of events that allows somebody to see themselves in the pains, desires, and transformation of another relatable human being, thus increasing their receptiveness to change. Out of all the stories I teach, this is the one that leaders, teams, salespeople, and entrepreneurs fixate on learning. Because they all know that their ability to inspire change and move people to action is the difference between success and failure.

Selling a product or service? Rallying your team around a common purpose? Trying to gain buy-in for your idea? You are selling change, my friend. When I say "change," I mean somebody making a conscious decision to depart from a specific set of behaviors (and thus, habits) that have formed their current reality, and substituting them for ones that directly map to their desired reality.

There's just one problem. As we've already learned, change is difficult. If the perceived cost of making change outweighs the perceived cost of sitting in the status quo, then human beings will opt for the easy way out and take the path of least resistance. Quite simply, it's in our nature. While I don't subscribe to the idea of New Year's resolutions, they perfectly explain what I mean.

How many times have you announced your desire to get into the best shape of your life on January 1, only to find your shiny new gym membership gathering dust by February? Though you start your journey with excitement, the appeal of returning to your old self grows as the perceived cost of making lasting change gradually reveals itself. This leads to taking the path of least resistance and quietly quitting. According to Columbia University, nearly half of all Americans make New Year's resolutions, yet only 25 percent of people stay committed to them after thirty days, and less than 10 percent actually accomplish their desires. So, even if somebody wants change, why is it so difficult to build momentum and realize one's desires?

Donald Edmondson, associate professor of behavioral medicine at Columbia's Irving Medical Center, points out how behavioral scientists are discovering that desires may be more easily achieved if they are linked to benefits that surpass self-interest. He highlights an effective technique used by healthcare workers for sparking true behavioral change, "motivational interviewing." This is grounded in the thesis that when people uncover the core motivation behind their desire and discover how their current behaviors are incongruent with achieving it, change is ignited. He goes on to give the example of somebody realizing that their poor diet and sedentary behavior are at odds with their desire for better health and core motivation of playing in the yard with their grandchildren. As Edmondson suggests, while a desire for better health is noble, a core motivation that goes beyond self-interest is what results in true change.[33]

Let me hit you with an example. Remember the skinny little Indian kid who hated the cold and would do anything to get out of his Saturday swimming lesson? My relationship with the cold clung to me for decades, until it didn't. Once it hit me that the cost of doing nothing would be more painful than making change, everything began to shift. I ensured my desire for bulletproof immunity was rooted in the core motivation of being an impactful father, husband, and leader. The result? Engaging in regular cold plunging, making the behavior habitual and reinforcing my new identity. A desire detached from an unhealthy ego state and an underlying motivation that goes beyond self-interest has the ability to change the trajectory of your life.

What does this mean for you? In everyday conversations, when you uncover what someone truly desires, reveal their core motivations, and shine a metaphorical light on the gap between those desires and their current actions, the magic unfolds. The catalyst for moving people to action is a well-intentioned change agent: a social proof story that triggers trust.

That said, not all social proof is created equal, and not every piece of social proof is a story. Among the different leaders, teams, and entrepreneurs I've trained, the common misconception lies in their belief that the testimonials on their company's website are stories, the case studies they send to prospects are stories, and the reviews they have from customers that vouch for them and their expertise are also stories. This is not the case.

While all of these vehicles may offer powerful insights and increase one's credibility stock, none of them are stories in my eyes. At a fundamental level, they're all missing one thing: connective tissue. This is why a connection-focused social proof story is a true trust accelerator. When the right story is shared at the right time, with the right person, our Three C's of Trust (connection, character, and competence) organically come to fruition. As you will learn, social proof that unfolds in the form of a story should contain a specific framework and set of key ingredients. More on this shortly.

A SOCIAL PROOF STORY: EXAMPLE

Trying to raise money for your cause? Want to motivate somebody in your team to embody a new behavior? Selling your product or service to a skeptical prospect? If you're nodding, then the social proof story is for you. Let's walk through a live example of what this story looks like in practice. Then we'll dissect it, analyze it, and give you the tools you need to create your own.

Let's assume you're a busy mid-level manager who's running a seven-person sales development team (even if this doesn't describe your current role or responsibilities, stay with me, things are about to get juicy). Your salespeople's job is to engage in out-bound sales activity and book qualified meetings that result in a prospect showing up for a meaningful conversation with one of your company's account executives. Alas, there's a problem. Your prospects are bored of receiving the same vanilla, predictable, and soulless messages—and they're begging for someone to flip the script and capture their attention by doing something different.

You want to give the people what they want and believe video prospecting through social media is the answer. But here's the problem, Jessica on your team has convinced herself otherwise and believes video "doesn't work."

Even though Jessica is struggling to hit her number this quarter, she's resistant to change—held back by her fear around sending sixty-second videos to prospects. Video could be her ticket to success, yet the perceived effort of testing your hypothesis is currently outweighing the cost of doing nothing at all. The path of least resistance is calling Jessica's name. Change is hard, remember?

Shoving your perspective down her throat will do nothing but increase resistance. Instead, you begin by asking conscious questions and make Jessica feel significant in your presence. This paves the way for you to embed a social proof story in your conversation. The goal? To accelerate trust, increase her receptiveness to change, and help her achieve more of what she desires. Not only will this help you develop a trusted relationship, but an organic byproduct will be you receiving more of what you desire—in this case, building a reputation for being the type of leader who creates leaders and eventually joining the C-suite at your company.

You begin by asking, "Jessica, what would it take for you to hit your quarterly quota?" Silence. You say nothing and create a safe space for reflection. Jessica sits there pondering your question, crosses her arms, and eventually breaks the silence by outlining her thought process on how she can hit her number. At the end, she says something that prompts you to ask a follow-up Storyworthy Question: ". . . and we all know video prospecting doesn't work." You pause for a moment, lean in with curiosity, and ask, "Can you tell me more about that?" As Jessica opens up and shares her perspective—rooted in her own reality—you listen deeply, without judgment, without interrupting. In doing so, you earn the opportunity to share your social proof story.

You take a beat and say, "Funny enough, Jeremy was in a similar space back in 2020, when he was a sales development representative who had one thing on his mind: hitting quota so he could buy his dad a once-in-a-lifetime trip to South Africa for his birthday.

"One Friday morning, I remember having a coffee with Jeremy over at Burky's, and he said, 'I've tried everything! Well, everything but cold calling, but that's so 1980s . . . we all know cold calling doesn't work. If I can't turn things around, it's going to get ugly!' I remember how stressed Jeremy was that day and the crippling anxiety he felt about the potential of being placed on a performance improvement plan (PIP).

"When we dug deeper into Jeremy's thought process, something incredible happened. He realized that to hit his quota, he needed to question his deepest convictions. It turns out, they were rooted in fear. To get different results, he needed to do something different.

"Jeremy didn't just hit his quota; he beat it by 17.4 percent, all because he tried something new: cold calling! Not only did this help him buy his father that holiday to South Africa and avoid a PIP, but today, Jeremy is a leader at our sister company.

"Here's why I'm telling you this: From my ten years inside the business, I've noticed one thing about those who hit their goals. They get comfortable with being uncomfortable.

What inside of Jeremy's story resonates with you the most?"

THE SOCIAL PROOF STORY:
THE FOUR-STEP STORY FRAMEWORK

Before we dissect the story I just shared, let's remind ourselves of what a social proof story is exactly. As you recall, I define it as a narrative that unfolds in a sequential series of events that allows somebody to see themselves in the pains, desires, and transformation of another relatable human being, thus increasing their receptiveness to change. Our example embodies exactly this.

Whoever you are reading this, the social proof story will help you sell yourself, an idea, product, or service using the art of storytelling in any conversation, meeting, pitch, or presentation. In our example, you're guiding Jessica to internalize a new idea during a 1:1 conversation—so she can challenge her deepest convictions and engage in a new behavior that aligns with her true desires. Sparking imperfect action—the kind that builds momentum and drives real change—starts with an open, Jessica-centric conversation that meets her where she is today, without judgment.

When you tell somebody a story of a human being who is "just like them," who has gone from pain to glory (with as little friction as possible), not only will it help you build trust and reduce skepticism, but it'll help you be seen as a trusted guide (something we'll talk about in the next habit). Keeping this in mind, let's get into the weeds of our example and break down exactly what's happening in four simple steps.

Step 1: Don't start with a story. Start with a "pattern interrupt."

A "pattern interrupt," commonly attributed to Richard Bandler and John Grinder's neuro-linguistic programming (NLP) theory, refers to an interruption introduced to break an individual's state of being or habit.[34] For example, marketers work endlessly to "stop the scroll" when you're browsing the internet through interruptions such as eye-catching images, pain-driven copy, and more. Why? So you can give their content your undivided attention. In our context, this content is your upcoming story. As a reminder, here's the interrupt used in our example: "Jessica, what would it take for you to hit your quarterly quota?"

By asking a Storyworthy Question, you interrupt Jessica's existing thought process and spark creativity. For the remainder of this habit, we will refer to this as a **"hook."** Side note—did you notice the first four words used when framing the question? Dr. Zoe Chance, senior lecturer at Yale School of Management, coined this approach the "magic question."[35] The idea is to frame one's ask using the following words at the start: "What would it take..." This leaves the other person divulging a road map of exactly what needs to occur to make your desire a reality. In this case, it's your desire for uncovering Jessica's existing thought process around hitting her quota. A question like this allows her to move into problem-solving mode as she begins creatively brainstorming a solution.

The way I see it, a hook can be a statement, statistic, analogy, or question that triggers curiosity, stimulates an internal question in the listener's mind, and initiates a search for an answer. When it comes to that search, I believe we already have the answer within us. Revealing an answer lies in finding solitude, creating the space to tap into our intuition, and listening without bias. However, we live in an imperfect world, and instead of going inward in times of uncertainty, human beings tend to look externally for validation. This isn't a new phenomenon.

In Dr. Robert Cialdini's book, *Influence: The Psychology of Persuasion*, he highlights Social Proof as his sixth principle of influence.[36] Cialdini believes that when people are feeling a sense of uncertainty, they look externally for answers and validation from people "just like them." In our case, your story for Jessica about Jeremy (somebody similar to her) could provide her with an external answer to the internal question she's asking herself: What steps do

I need to take in order to hit my quarterly quota? The ultimate goal is to help her tap into her inner voice, stop operating out of fear, and arrive at her own conclusion for how to best move forward.

However, here's the key: your hook must be succinct. How long is "succinct," you ask? I invite you to use the scenario, person, and setting in question as context. Just keep the following in mind: a hook is designed to pique curiosity so your story receives the attention it deserves. In light of that, less is more. Ensure your hook is no shorter than it should be and no longer than it needs to be.

Finally, remember that our focus is on stimulating a question in Jessica's mind rather than giving unsolicited advice rooted in our perception of the world. Here's what's unfolding when you do this with intention. Firstly, neuroplasticity, which is seen as our brain's ability to adapt, change, or grow neural networks—and in our case, create structural changes as a result of learning—is in full force.[37]

According to an article in *Government Executive*, insightful open-ended questions force new insights and serve as a catalyst for change. Through my lens, this is no different to asking Storyworthy Questions. Secondly, by applying this line of thinking to our context, when you lead with a hook in the form of a Storyworthy Question, our brains are activated as they enter reflection mode and release a neurochemical called serotonin, which helps us relax. This encourages insight gathering from all parts of the brain, allowing for more "aha moments" than if you were to interject with your perspective. Meaning, just barking orders at Jessica and giving her your opinion, because "you know best," won't have the impact you desire.

As the brain works toward finding a solution to the question, new neuronal connections begin to form. As serotonin is released, insights rush to the person you're trying to connect with and a search for a solution is activated. Change has officially been inspired.[38]

Cool, right? But will that change be long-lasting? That depends on Jessica's ability to identify her core motivation and be loyal to her future self, alongside you caring about what she's emotionally invested in through accountability.

So, what happens after you deliver this succinct hook? In Jessica's response, she mentions the idea of video prospecting, yet instantly starts to talk herself out of it. While she doesn't admit it out loud, crossing her arms signals closed body language and is evidence of her internal resistance. As she engages in this reactive behavior, you don't interrupt her. You let her finish talking and ask her to tell you more. As you ask this judgment-free question with the driving force of curiosity (versus interjecting with your opinion), you find the perfect point in the conversation to segue into your story.

Step 2: Segue into your story
(context, conflict, change, conclusion)

What's the most impactful way to start your story? With a relatable main character who has a similar desire and resembles the DNA of the human being you're trying to connect with. By beginning with **"context,"** you'll be able to further earn Jessica's attention and patience for listening to the rest of your story. Why? Because you've made it about her, not about you. You are subtly showing her that you're interested in what she's emotionally invested in. Empathy at its best. Here's what that looked like:

"Funny enough, Jeremy was in a similar space back in 2020, when he was a sales development representative who had one thing on his mind: hitting quota so he could buy his dad a once-in-a-lifetime trip to South Africa for his birthday."

Check out the depth of this brief context setting. Main character? Jeremy. Time? 2020. DNA? A sales development representative just like Jessica. Desire? Hitting quota. Core motivation? Buying his father a trip to South Africa. When delivered in a conversational tone and with this level of intricacy, connection is an organic byproduct.

Enter the villain in the eyes of Jeremy: the fear of trying something new. As we introduce **"conflict"** into the story, we not only aim to sustain attention, but we attempt to evoke emotion. In this moment, as you paint a vivid picture of your previous chat with Jeremy at the local coffee shop, Jessica begins to mentally place herself in the same scene that's been painted:

"One Friday morning, I remember having a coffee with Jeremy over at Burky's, and he said, 'I've tried everything! Well, everything but cold calling, but that's so 1980s . . . we all know cold calling doesn't work. If I can't turn things around, it's going to get ugly!' I remember how stressed Jeremy was that day and the crippling anxiety he felt about the potential of being placed on a PIP."

Words such as "stressed" and "crippling anxiety" are designed to connect with Jessica beyond the surface. The key lies in using the exact language that Jeremy used to describe his pain to increase your likelihood of resonating with Jessica's current internal state. This is what will help her lean in and become more emotionally invested in your story.

Interestingly, even though Jeremy's problem has nothing to do with video prospecting, Jessica connects to the source of his pain: the fear of trying something new. Contrary to what you may believe, when you're able to connect to the source of somebody's pain, people become invested in the main character's journey, versus the specific destination. It's why I'm obsessed with the *Rocky* and *Creed* franchises. While I have no desire to be a boxing world champion, I do care about the journey of realizing my own greatness. Furthermore, by raising the stakes of your story and mentioning what will happen to Jeremy professionally if he doesn't ignite change (being put on a PIP). You allow your narrative to sustain attention.

Next up, it's Jeremy's moment of **"change,"** otherwise seen as his "aha moment." As we revisit this event inside of the story, notice how Jeremy realizes all on his own what is holding him back. Also look carefully at the language used. "We" displays a partnership, and "he" ensures you take the spotlight off you, allowing you to be seen as a trusted guide. Remember, the goal is for the person you're trying to connect with to see themselves in the pains, desires, and transformation of the main character of your story. When done right, this will inspire change and allow them to become the hero of their own. If you hijack this intention and make you, your product, service, or idea front and center, then you'll dilute trust, dampen your influence, and create a disconnect. As they say, "Be the guide, not the guru." Here's what you said in our example:

"When we dug deeper into Jeremy's thought process, something incredible happened. He realized that to hit his quota, he needed to question his deepest convictions. It turns out, they were rooted in fear. To get different results, he needed to do something different."

This point of inflection is the catalyst for Jeremy's transformation. Not only can this part of the story pique Jessica's curiosity for learning about how things ended for him, but it will give her permission to realize or acknowledge what's driving her own belief around video prospecting. As long as her nervous system feels safe in doing so, this could lead to an open and vulnerable conversation about what's truly holding her back.

Jeremy has officially reached the promised land. Quite simply, this is the **"conclusion"** of the story:

"Jeremy didn't just hit his quota; he beat it by 17.4 percent, all because he tried something new: cold calling! Not only did this help him buy his father that holiday to South Africa and avoid a PIP, but today, Jeremy is a leader at our sister company."

Notice how we use the exact number of 17.4 percent? Specificity breeds believability, whereas round, whole numbers often sound too good to be true. And not only does this resolution show Jeremy slaying his villain (fear) by trying something new (cold calling) and achieving his desire (hitting quota), but it shows him being able to buy his father a trip abroad (his core motivation). Finally, by showing where Jeremy is today, you are future-pacing Jessica to a world where she gets to see what's possible for her if she perseveres. As they say, "You can't be what you can't see."

Once again, this story's ending doesn't make you look like a helicopter leader who swooped in to save the day. Instead, it shows Jeremy transforming himself into the leader he knew he would always become. Jeremy is the hero; you are the trusted guide.

Up next is step 3, ensuring your story is relevant to the person you're trying to serve.

Step 3: Tie the core message of your story
back to the human being opposite you

How do you do this? By saying your version of "Here's why this matters to our conversation . . ." However, here's what most people miss. You must ensure that what comes out of your mouth afterward ties back to the purpose of the conversation or the problem you're trying to solve. This adds business value and guarantees **"impact."** Not only will your listener receive a meaningful takeaway, but your story will plant the seed of change. Here's how you did this in our example:

"Here's why I'm telling you this: From my ten years inside the business, I've noticed one thing about those who hit their goals. They get comfortable with being uncomfortable."

The first six words allow you to perfectly segue into the core message of your story. As you can see, you also provide Jessica with your unique perspective. That's fine to do, but tread with caution and resist providing a solution. Inside this step, the goal is to help Jessica come to the realization (all on her own) that her current behavior is at odds with her desires. To wrap things up in a pretty little bow, you ended with a conscious question.

Step 4: Ask a conscious question

Ending with a **"conscious question"** in the form of a Storyworthy Question begins a two-way dialogue grounded in openness and creativity. In the case of our example, here's what that looks like: "What inside of Jeremy's story resonates with you the most?"

The beauty of this moment is that Jessica feels safe enough to admit her fear of video prospecting and opens up with a vulnerable story about the core motivation behind her desire— marking the beginning of a trusted relationship. Eventually, she ends up formulating her own plan of action, which includes video prospecting, without your active intervention. Remember, the goal of a social proof story is not to persuade, convince, or beg Jessica to change her mind. Such behavior would be rooted in lack, fear, or scarcity and signal reactiveness. The goal is to positively affect how Jessica thinks, behaves, and acts, so she can get one step closer to her desires. This is how you achieve limitless influence.

PRACTICE: SHARE SOCIAL PROOF IN THE FORM OF A STORY
Okay, my friend, by breaking down our example, you've uncovered a simple four-step story framework for crafting your very own social proof story:

- Step 1: Hook
- Step 2: Story (context, conflict, change, conclusion)
- Step 3: Impact
- Step 4: Conscious Question

To simply reinforce what we've just learned, let's highlight each step once more.

Step 1: Hook. This should trigger curiosity, pose an internal question in the listener's mind that cannot remain unanswered, and allow your story to receive the attention it deserves.

Step 2: Story. Hit them with brief context and introduce a relatable main character with a specific desire. Then, unveil the villain creating the conflict that's preventing the main character (and your conversation partner) from reaching the promised land. Next up, change: the main character experiences an "aha moment" that reshapes their perspective and drives change. Finally, conclude your story and give the listener a resolution; unveil the transformation as the main character goes from pain to glory. Remember, you aren't the hero; you are the trusted guide.

Step 3: Impact. Tie your core message back to the listener and illuminate that their current behavior is at odds with their desires without preaching.

Step 4: Ask a conscious question that stimulates an open two-way dialogue.

So, now what?

I invite you to digest the above and begin creating your very own social proof story.

Now, as you can imagine, the social proof story isn't just applicable to leaders inspiring change among their direct reports. It can be used in any scenario where you're selling yourself, your idea, product, or service (a.k.a. change).

To access a simple one-page worksheet that guides you in creating your own social proof story, along with an example tailored for someone selling a product or service to a potential or existing customer, head to theravirajani.com/bookresources.

One final thing to note. In our example where you saw the four-step framework in action, the story takes approximately two minutes or less to deliver. Don't forget that the longer your story, the more mental capacity you are requesting from your listener. For those dipping their toes into the waters of influential storytelling, I recommend creating a "minimum viable story" and testing it immediately in low-stakes scenarios to start the process of iteration. Over time, you can craft more than one social proof story and create your very own "Story Bank." To collapse time on this journey, ensure your story contains five simple ingredients.

THE A.C.O.R.N CHECKLIST—FIVE INGREDIENTS OF A SOCIAL PROOF STORY

Ralph Waldo Emerson once said, "The creation of a thousand forests is in one acorn." When I stumbled upon these words, it hit me. The creation of a thousand relationships is in one story. In light of this, allow me to introduce you to the ACORN checklist.

After many iterations, this checklist includes just five simple questions to ask yourself to ensure you have all the ingredients of a compelling social proof story without analysis paralysis. In practice, are there actually more than five? Yes, of course. But I don't want you to get infobese and suffocate your ability to take imperfect action. Let's keep things simple and focus on progress over perfection. As you're crafting your own story, ask yourself the following five questions to ensure you're on the right track.

Does your story . . .

> A – *Actively interrupt somebody's trail of thought (i.e., have a hook)?*
>
> C – *Contain a story arc (i.e., display context, conflict, change, conclusion)?*
>
> O – *Organically add business value (i.e., showcase impact)?*
>
> R – *Revive a two-way dialogue (i.e., end with a conscious question)?*
>
> N – *Noticeably make your main character the hero (i.e., show you as the guide, not the guru)?*

Simple, right? A yes or no answer to each of these questions will help you determine if you have the five key ingredients needed to create an influential social proof story. Now, the million-dollar question is this: Once you're ready to test your story out in the wild, how will you know when success has been achieved?

THE SOCIAL PROOF STORY ACID TEST

How do you know what "good" looks like, and how do you measure the success of your story? There are three potential outcomes.

Outcome 1: The Holy Grail. The law of reciprocity holds. As you share a connection-focused story that displays high levels of empathy, the other person feels compelled to exchange a story in return due to the psychological safety created.

Outcome 2: The Halfway House. You spark intrigue, yet resistance is still rife. As a result, they ask a follow-up question on a specific part of your story that captured their attention, but with clear skepticism. This shows openness, yet their guard is still up, and some reluctance remains. Not a bad place to be—honor where they're at and simply see this as data for the next iteration of your story.

Outcome 3: The Disconnect. Your story was a "dud," and they quickly move on or disregard it, holding on to their deepest conviction with a death grip. Own the imperfect moment and see this as an opportunity for connection (as we delved into in Habit 3). Not only can this moment humanize you and the conversation, but it can lead to an incredible relationship rooted in vulnerability. This isn't a bad place to be either; uncover what led to this outcome, seek feedback on what you've "missed or misunderstood," and focus on creating the next iteration of your story.

As you can see, your story is meant to be built first, then polished later. It's always evolving—and that's the beauty of it. When implemented with intention, a story rooted in social proof accelerates trust and inspires change. Still don't believe me? Let's unpack some of the research to see what it says about this philosophy.

SOCIAL PROOF: POUR EMOTIVE FUEL ON THE FIRE OF CHANGE
I'm not here to walk you through *all* of the science of storytelling; there are enough books out there already doing that. Instead, I'd like to highlight compelling research on why stories inspire change.

Allow me to introduce you to Paul Zak, an American neuroscientist whose lab pioneered the behavioral study of oxytocin, otherwise known as the love or bonding hormone. His team's work proved that when the brain synthesizes this neurochemical, people are considered more trustworthy, generous, and charitable, in turn increasing one's likelihood of engaging in cooperative behaviors.[39]

Fascinatingly, Zak's lab wondered if they could "hack" the oxytocin system with the goal of motivating participants to engage in cooperative behaviors. To test this, they wanted to see if a narrative shot on video, rather than a face-to-face interaction, would cause the brain to make oxytocin. By taking blood draws both before and after the narrative, and measuring the oxytocin levels of the participants, here's what they found. Character-led stories consistently stimulate oxytocin. Furthermore, higher levels of oxytocin predicted how much people were willing to engage in the target cooperative behavior: helping another human being. In this case, it was donating money to the charity in the video. What does this mean for you? Remember, your social proof story needs a relatable human being as a main character. If this is missing from the context of your story, your ability to stimulate oxytocin—and make someone receptive to change—will be nearly nonexistent.

In following studies, Zak's research (backed by the US Department of Defense) dug deeper into why stories inspire action in the form of voluntary cooperation. They discovered this: to inspire a desire to help others, a story must first sustain attention. This is done by developing tension in the narrative, which in our case boils down to ensuring clear conflict through the inclusion of a villain in your story.

Zak found that if a story creates tension, then it's likely a listener will come to share the emotions of the characters in it, and after it ends, they may even continue to mimic the feelings and behaviors of those characters. For example, in our case, as Jessica was able to resonate with Jeremy's villain, it sparked an emotion and caused her to give you her full attention. The result? After the story, she was open to an honest conversation about trying something different and embodying a new behavior (just like Jeremy did).

Zak's research also found that character-driven stories containing emotional content enhance both comprehension of the speaker's key points and the listener's recall weeks afterward. The more emotion you can evoke in the conflict of your story, the more likely it will be sticky, memorable, and a springboard for action (even weeks or months later). As Zak goes on to suggest, when you want to inspire, start with a story of human struggle and end with a triumph. If you learned nothing else in this chapter, this simple nugget of wisdom will ensure you build the momentum you need to craft your first social proof story.

As you continue your ascent to unconscious competence with this habit, know that a filthy and disgusting amount of practice is required for this to feel natural and instinctive. Remember, amateurs wing it; professionals make you feel like they're winging it. There's a difference. Script your story, practice it in low-stakes scenarios, iterate, and graduate to high-stakes scenarios. Not only will this help you sound conversational, insert your unique voice, and free up mental space to have fun with it, but it will also ensure you can cut your story down to exactly the right length to have the impact you desire. Remember, mastery means learning to delay gratification.

In a real-life conversation, you may not get through your story entirely without being interrupted. When delivering a presentation, you may forget to tie your core message back to the audience. Or in a 1:1 meeting with a team member, you might spend too much time setting context and forget parts of your conclusion. That's okay, my friend, that's okay. This is a process. The key is for you to follow the framework, create freedom in the framework, and then break it in accordance with your energy, swagger, and personality. Own the framework—don't let it own you. There are no trophies here for flawless outcomes, only for taking imperfect action. When it's all said and done, you'll earn the opportunity to become a trusted guide in the eyes of the person you're trying to impact. And that is exactly where we're headed next.

THE HIGHLIGHT REEL

1. Selling a product or service? Rallying your team around a common purpose? Trying to gain buy-in for your idea? You are selling change.
2. A social proof story is a narrative that unfolds in a sequential series of events that allows somebody to see themselves in the pains, desires, and transformation of another relatable human being, thus increasing their receptiveness to change.
3. Your story should unfold within a simple four-step framework: Hook, Story (context, conflict, change, conclusion), Impact, and Conscious Question. When listeners see themselves in someone "just like them," your story becomes a powerful agent for change.
4. If everything else fails, start with a story of human struggle and end with a triumph.
5. Create a minimum viable story and instantly test it in low-stakes scenarios. Practice, tweak, and iterate

like your life depends on it, so you can shine in high-stakes scenarios.

BECOME THE TRUSTED GUIDE

A short-term mindset kills long-term reputation.

Look around you. Look left. Look right. Now look straight ahead. What do you see? Are people rushing from one meeting to the next? Do they have their heads mindlessly buried in their smartphones? Is it possible that they're subconsciously chasing a desire for "more," without a clear sense of purpose? When we engage in such actions, one phrase comes to mind: reactive behavior. As we've already acknowledged, when we are reactive, quite simply, we operate from a place of lack, fear, or scarcity, while adopting a short-term mindset.

Rushing a prospect or customer through a buying decision because you crave that commission check? Reactive behavior. Hoarding wisdom from your direct report to create a sense of reliance because you don't want them to leave you? Reactive behavior. "Forgetting" to tell your teammate about the new internal managerial opportunity because you want to maintain a superior status? Reactive behavior. You get the picture, right?

A short-term mindset kills long-term reputation and your ability to build trusted relationships. As I see it, the pull of instant gratification is what fuels reactive behavior. And as we have already discussed throughout this book, instant gratification is the villain in our story. So, the question is how can we slay our villain once and for all? By embodying the role of a trusted guide.

Being a trusted guide is about living a lifestyle where one has a long-term outlook, operates with a service mindset, and competently helps others realize their desires, without self-interest. Now, I'm not asking you to lose sight of your desires and become passive in your approach—quite the contrary. Instead, I'm inviting you to revisit what you learned when you began your journey inside this book. Yes, unapologetically pursue desires that are driven by your authentic self and feel abundant by nature; at the same time, surrender the need for them to come to fruition. When you develop self-trust, wash away the smell of desperation from your aura, and release your expectations of how you want things to look—without losing sight of your vision—that's when abundance will find you.

The moment we engage in reactive behavior, short-termism has taken the driver's seat. And when a short-term mindset is evident, you're instantly at odds with the lifestyle of a trusted guide. However, on the other side is a "contrarian approach," which results in a different reality. Here's what that looks like in practice.

Instead of rushing a prospect or customer through a buying decision, you'll slow down, ask conscious questions, and prescribe a solution that's best for them, versus one that solely serves your bank balance. Instead of holding back your nuggets of wisdom from the number two on your team, you'll share freely and openly, knowing that "leaders create leaders" (as my friend and mentor Gerard Adams likes to say). And instead of "forgetting" to tell your friend at work about the new internal managerial position that would be perfect for them, you share this knowledge with joy, knowing that what's meant for you will never pass you by and that life is not a zero-sum game. This is what being a trusted guide is about. Removing the disease of scarcity from your behavior, embracing a marathon mindset, and realizing that life is happening for you, not to you.

Business is not a 100-meter sprint. If it were, transactional behavior, hidden agendas, and a self-serving attitude would result in long-term fulfillment. Business is a lifelong marathon. Intentionality, integrity, and transparency—when this is your norm, you'll run that race earning relationship currency as you go and cultivate a reputation that stands the test of time.

In this habit, we will uncover three simple practices to help you embody the role of a trusted guide: the art of silent influence, how to answer a question you don't know without hurting your credibility, and the trusted guide message for stimulating a consultative conversation (even if you're struggling with imposter syndrome). When implemented, you'll positively affect how somebody thinks or behaves, guide them toward their desires, and achieve limitless influence.

PRACTICE: SILENT INFLUENCE—
EMBODY THE CHANGE YOU DESIRE TO SEE
"Dada, whatcha doing?" As a father to an inquisitive three-year-old (going on thirty-three) daughter, that is the number one question I receive on a daily basis. Every single day, my daughter is secretly watching me from a distance, observing my behavior, and carefully deciding whether or not it's worth imitating.

Remember Albert Bandura's Social Learning Theory (SLT) that we touched upon in Habit 2? In his 1977 book, *Social Learning Theory*, Bandura explains, "Most human behavior is learned observationally through modeling: from observing others one forms an idea of how new behaviors are performed, and on later occasions, this coded information serves as a guide for action."[40] Ultimately, Bandura's theory suggests that observation and modeling play a primary role in how and why humans learn. While not all observed behaviors are effectively learned, attention, retention, motor reproduction, and motivation are essential for one to benefit from social learning practices.

On the surface, this sounds intuitive. But here's the million-dollar question: Why do we lean on verbal commands as the primary path for igniting change in others? In my case with my daughter, she does what I do, not what I say. Here's a case in point.

It's 2024 and a stereotypically icy, fresh, and crisp winter morning in the UK—the perfect morning for a cold plunge followed by some breathwork. My routine is simple. I sit in my safe space, drown out the external noise, and allow my breath to be guided by Wim Hof.[41] Inhale through the nose, fill up my belly and chest with each breath, and follow up with a relaxed exhale through my mouth. Repeat thirty times, and on the thirtieth breath, I hold my breath for as long as I can. When my body is screaming at me for air, I inhale fully and hold for fifteen seconds before releasing. Two rounds of this normally does me nicely!

This morning, my daughter (who was a one-year-old at the time) seems fascinated with why her dad is breathing heavier than a horse. Halfway through my practice, she barges into the room like a puppy on skates and almost instantly a faint scent of milk breath enters my aura. As I pop one eye open, there she is, pleasantly invading my personal space, staring at me like I'm an alien from outer space. Looking confused and worried, she says, "Dada, um ga, ga ga?!" (Today, I'm convinced that was her way of asking "Dada, watcha doing?!" before she could string a sentence together.) I put her on my lap, finish up my practice, and get on with my day.

The next morning, déjà vu. There I was, eyes closed, crossed-legged and engaging in breathwork once again. Halfway through, my daughter barges into the room—same puppy-on-skates energy—and sits there at point blank range from my face with that same faint odor of milk breath. I pop one eye open with a smile. As she watches a series of intense breaths come out of my mouth, she says, "Dada, um ga, ga ga?!" I put her on my lap, finish up my practice, and get on with my day.

The next day, it is a different story. (What happened has been burned into my memory forever!) Eyes closed? Check. Wim Hof breathwork? Check. A circulation of milk breath in my aura? Nowhere to be smelled. I pop one eye open, and there's my little space invader, sitting on my wife's lap on the other side of the room. However, this time, there's no confused look on her face. Instead, she takes a deep breath in and exhales through her mouth with a twinkle in her eye, as though she was seeking my seal of approval. I was speechless. She wanted to be just like dada. In a state of shock, and feeling pretty self-righteous may I add, it hit me like a ton of bricks: for the rest of my life, my job wasn't to tell my daughter what to do; it was to show her who to be. A behavior, repeated consistently, formed a habit that was later imitated by my daughter without verbal instruction. This is the beautiful power of what I call "silent influence." This is a cutesy example I'm sharing with you, but don't get it twisted, my daughter also has a knack for imitating the behaviors I'm not so proud of. She models the good, the bad, *and* the ugly!

Here's why I'm telling you this.

If you tell your people to show up with passion and energy when on the phone with customers, yet you sound uninspired yourself, there's a disconnect. If you tell prospects you're a premium service but then act "cheap" during the buying experience, there's a disconnect. I believe this deeply in my core: people will do as you do, not as you say. Quite simply, your job is to stop telling and start showing. However, before trying to influence those around you, begin with the person staring back at you in the mirror: you. This is the person that will start this chain reaction. Here are my three steps for silent influence so you can usher people toward their desired reality.

- Step 1: Identify the behavior you want others to exhibit.
- Step 2: Pick a habit to facilitate this transformation (e.g., asking conscious questions or telling influential stories).
- Step 3: Reward others to reinforce the behavior at scale.

Let's walk through an example.

Let's say you want others to showcase more vulnerability in their client conversations because you know it will help them build more intimate relationships. Instead of beating the verbal drum of "Team, I want you to be more vulnerable as that's one of our core values . . . " try these three steps instead.

Step 1: Acknowledge that authentic vulnerability is the change you want to see, as this will help your people unlock more of what they truly desire, and in turn, it will support your company's top-line growth.

Step 2: Choose and implement your vehicle for change. For me, when it comes to inspiring vulnerability, there's no better way to do that than through the art of storytelling. As you've already learned, this can be a potent way to spark emotion, shift perspectives, and inspire change. Start by developing your first story using our four-step story framework from Habit 4: hook, story, impact, conscious question. However, this time, you're ensuring the moral of your story ties into the benefits of leading with vulnerability. Remember to say something along the lines of the following inside the "impact" element of your story: "Here's why this matters to you." As you implement this in the wild, this will ensure your story includes the one thing that's often missed in business storytelling: relevance. When your story includes a snackable lesson or takeaway that adds business value, it evokes empathy rather than sympathy. This is essential if you want to be seen as a trusted guide.

Step 3: As others observe your behavior and try it on for size, acknowledge and reward them to reinforce the change you wish to see. It doesn't have to be fancy or over the top. For example, it could be as simple as giving somebody a genuine compliment in public that makes them feel significant in your presence and like their contribution matters to the wider business. (Remember the ASI framework from Habit 3?) A study published by *Frontiers in Psychology* found that when employees received verbal praise, it created a sense of psychological ownership and affective commitment, leading to increased discretionary behaviors that benefit the organization.[42]

When these three steps are executed with intention, not only will your teammates, direct reports, and/or managers follow suit, but they will diffuse this behavior at scale within your organization. Cool, right?

Remember, my friend, congruence is everything. The moment you embody the behavior you want others to exhibit—both when people are watching and when they're not—you begin a personal transformation and amplify the power of your words, allowing your example to become a beacon of light for others. This serves as a North Star, guiding people toward their desires without preaching or offering unsolicited advice. Nonetheless, this isn't about emulating perfection. As we uncovered in previous chapters, not only is that exhausting and unachievable, but it suffocates connection. Remember when I said imperfection equals connection? Here's another case in point.

PRACTICE: OWN YOUR TRUTH—ANSWERING QUESTIONS YOU DON'T HAVE AN ANSWER FOR

Have you ever felt ashamed, embarrassed, or inadequate when asked a question you don't know the answer to? Maybe you secretly fear these moments in job interviews, client pitches, or high-stakes conversations. As a result, it suffocates your ability to communicate with credibility and confidence. But more importantly, it keeps you from being seen as a trusted guide by those you wish to serve. If you're nodding, then stay with me, friend.

Over the years, I've learned this: when we're asked a question we don't know the answer to in a high-stakes scenario, our personal relationship with authenticity is *tested*. In a basic sense, we have two options:

- **Option 1:** Lie—which is the pinnacle of reactive behavior, putting you out of integrity with yourself and breaking trust with the person in front of you.
- **Option 2:** Own your truth—which sparks a connection, shows a character of integrity and paradoxically signals competence; ultimately helping you display the Three C's of Trust.

What I've found is that people *want* to tell the truth. However, their fear of losing credibility and not being perceived as perfect gets in the way. Not only that, but they don't know what to say or how to say it without undermining someone's confidence in them. As a result, this perceived threat triggers a flurry of stress hormones that produce perfectly choreographed physiological changes. Tense muscles, sweaty palms, you name it. This cocktail of reactions to stress is otherwise known as the "fight or flight" response, designed to protect us from what it perceives as a life-threatening situation.[43] In our case, that's being seen as imperfect. The outcome? A knee-jerk reaction that dilutes your credibility stock.

But what if I told you that there is a way to answer questions you don't know in a strategic and authentic manner, while still being seen as a trusted guide? Let's walk through an example. Picture this: you've just delivered the biggest client pitch of your life, and now you're knee-deep in Q&A.

All of a sudden, the CFO—who's been quiet the entire conversation—hits you with a difficult question that you don't have an answer to. The room goes silent, and the spotlight is on you. You feel an overwhelming sense of pressure as you are somebody who's "supposed" to have an answer. So, what do you do?

Instead of deflecting, making up an answer, or stalling, you take a beat and say:

"Alex, that's a really good question that I don't have an answer for. What I'm going to do is this: after our conversation, I'll do some digging to find you the answer, and if that fails, I will introduce you to the right person who can. Does that sound fair enough?" The outcome? An instant acceleration of trust. Depending on what feels right for you and your unique voice, you could even start with, "Alex, that's a really good question that's outside of my area of expertise. . ." Make it your own.

The magic lies in your tone, warmth, and using an upward inflection (yup, once again) at the end to ensure it sounds like a curious question versus an aggressive statement. And then, the key lies in your follow-up, response time, and ability to become the "expert in finding the expert." This is what a trusted guide does. They confidently own their competency boundaries. They don't operate from a place of lack, fear, or scarcity. And they've let go of the need to be seen as the white knight—that kind of response would be considered reactive behavior. When you own your truth, stay in your zone of genius, and show your resourcefulness, that's when you add value and build a trusted relationship by ensuring your ego isn't a bottleneck in helping somebody get closer to their desires. Contrary to what you might believe, this signals true competence.

When asked a question you don't know, remember this: admitting you don't have all of the answers, showcasing vulnerability, and being transparent is how you'll be seen as a trusted guide, simultaneously giving others permission to do exactly the same. Not only does this allow you to indirectly unlock the art of silent influence once again, but it will help you humanize any and every conversation. Whether it's a pricing discussion with a buyer, a job interview with your future leader, or a conversation with a strategic partner, remember that long-term relationships are built on one thing and one thing only: trust.

Throughout my work, I've noticed something consistent across the board when it comes to embodying the role of a trusted guide. When someone is selling themselves or their idea, product, or service to somebody they believe has more experience, expertise, or perceived credibility, they often dilute their true nature and become subservient. "But, Ravi, how am I supposed to build a trusted relationship with executives, leaders, and those who have been in the game longer than me?" I've got you, my friend. Firstly, I need you to know that they are a human being, just like you. They brush their teeth in the morning, just like you. They have been hurt, just like you. And they too experience moments of inadequacy, just like you. This is a part of the human experience. Secondly, to get practical, allow me to introduce you to a little something called "The Trusted Guide Message" so you can build rapport with those you've secretly put on a pedestal.

PRACTICE: THE TRUSTED GUIDE MESSAGE—SPARK A CONSULTATIVE CONVERSATION

One cold morning in London over a decade ago, I walked onto the trading floor, sat down at my desk, and felt a sense of inner peace before the markets opened. Why? As I looked left and right, nobody from my team had arrived yet. I cracked a smile and knew I'd been gifted the perfect opportunity to get a head start on my day without distraction.

As I headed to the printer to grab and inhale an overview of what happened to the markets overnight in Asia, I passed my mentor's desk, and among his tower of screen monitors, a bunch of bright yellow sticky notes caught my eye. I'd seen them before from afar, but today, I had the chance to get nosy and see them up close! After glancing behind me to make sure nobody was watching, I quickly snatched one of the sticky notes, cupped it in the palm of my hand, and took a closer look. It read, *Tell them something they didn't know before they spoke to you.* Secretly having hoped for more, I returned the note and sat back down at my desk, feeling confused. In hindsight, two words sum up that simple yellow sticky note: pure genius. But what on earth did these eleven words even mean?

As a starry-eyed graduate, I often wondered, "Ravi, what value are you going to add to a seasoned business leader with decades more experience and expertise than you?" Prior to walking into client pitches, presentations, and meetings, this question would often plague my mind like an overplayed song on the radio. Everything changed when I realized that sticky note's true meaning. My job wasn't to try and outshine somebody's hard-earned expertise. Instead, my job was to show up with a unique perspective that illuminated blind spots, share "pattern interrupting" insights that captured attention, and reveal trends from people "just like them" that could shape their future decisions. All I needed to do was teach them something they didn't know before they spoke to me, in order to be viewed on equal footing and spark a strategic two-way dialogue without resistance. This would help me earn the chance to solve their business problems and be seen as their trusted guide. Looking back, this simple moment on the trading floor is the inspiration for what I teach today: The Trusted Guide Message. Let me show you what it looks like in practice.

It's early 2023, and I'm on a Zoom call with a commercial leader from a SaaS company headquartered in Singapore. After we get the formalities out of the way, I say something along the lines of (refined for teaching purposes): "Would you be open to hearing about three trends I'm seeing right now in the SaaS space, specifically for revenue leaders looking to shorten their sales cycle? I'd also love to hear your perspective and see if there's anything I've missed or misunderstood."

From client feedback, market research, and conversations with peers, I distill my findings into three specific trends, weave in my point of view, and end with a thoughtful question along the lines of: "I saw you nodding when I mentioned the final trend; could you help me understand what connected with you the most?" A collaborative, consultative, and strategic conversation ensued. He instantly saw me as somebody "just like him"—not another speaker or trainer out to make a quick buck. In the end, he hired me to teach his global sales and customer success teams the art of influential storytelling.

Here's what worked for me in that moment. Connection—I used the same language his peers and internal team used to describe their pains and desires, showing that I care about what he was emotionally invested in (our definition of empathy). Character—I was well-prepared and well-researched, telling him a positive story about my value system. As they say, how you do one thing is how you do everything. Competence—I was able to have a strategic conversation, signaling expertise and increasing my credibility stock. And there we have the Three C's of Trust. When this trifecta is present, beautiful things unfold. Whether or not I "won" the deal was irrelevant. Did I want to help solve his problem through my services? Of course. Was I tied to this outcome? No. I knew that everything was happening for me, not to me. The goal was simple: to earn the opportunity to become his trusted guide and find his company a solution, with or without me. This is how you build a business relationship that lasts.

In this instance, we're talking about me selling a service. But the trusted guide message can be used by anybody trying to increase their influence, gain equal footing in a conversation, and communicate for trust.

Check out the free resources page over at theravirajani.com/bookresources to grab a template for creating your own Trusted Guide Message and applying it to your specific context.

Ultimately, it all boils down to the following process.

THE THREE-STEP TRUSTED GUIDE MESSAGE

Here's the three-step framework in a nutshell:

- Step 1: Ask a permission-based Factworthy Question (to invite collaboration).
- Step 2: Insert your wisdom (to signal competence).
- Step 3: Ask a Storyworthy Question (to stimulate a consultative conversation).

Step 1: Ask a permission-based Factworthy Question (to invite collaboration)

As discussed in Habit 2, a Factworthy Question (when used in the right context) helps you receive an intentionally limited response that may allow you to gain instant clarity on the direction and progression of a conversation. These aren't good or bad questions; they simply need to be used at the right time. This is that time. In any case, taking inspiration from our example, here's a template for you to try on for size when asking a Factworthy Question with the goal of inviting a collaborative conversation:

> *"Would you be open to hearing about three [ideas/*
> *trends/patterns] I'm currently seeing circulate the*
> *[insert industry] space for [insert job title for people*
> *'just like them'] who also want to [insert their desire]?*
> *I'd also love to hear your perspective and see if there's*
> *anything I've missed or misunderstood."*

Our initial permission-based question uses the word "open." In my experience, this approach is effective at lowering resistance and eliciting a "yes" from your conversation partner because of its collaborative and warm nature. Alternatively, you could use the word "opposed," which can subtly disarm someone and encourage cooperative behavior. Remember, context is everything. That said, don't just take my word for it—try both options and see which one fits your swagger, energy, and personality. And if neither lands, create a permission-based Factworthy Question that aligns with you.

Next, we mention three ideas, trends, or patterns. Not two, not one, not five. Why? Because three is seen as the smallest number of elements required to form a pattern, due to this being the minimum amount that can establish a sequence. The first two elements? They set up an expectation, while the third element either confirms or breaks this expectation, in turn creating a pattern.[44] Think about it, the three little pigs, the three wise men, the three musketeers—they all point to one thing. The number three is sticky, memorable, and helps support recall during a conversation.

Next up, by calling out people "just like them" and honing in on their desire, you trigger curiosity and naturally capture their attention, as you've made it all about them (not you). However, your final sentence is where the beauty lies: "I'd also love to hear your perspective and see if there's anything I've missed or misunderstood." By seeking somebody's perspective, you are showing them that you value their expertise and opinion, thus increasing both their willingness to be collaborative and the chances of you learning something new that you can bring to future conversations. Furthermore, when somebody explicitly or implicitly agrees to this, it incentivizes them to give you their undivided attention, as they will be looking to provide a thoughtful perspective based on your commentary. Also, by ending with the following words, you tell somebody you're open to being corrected, showcase vulnerability, and instantly humanize the conversation: ". . . and see if there's anything I've missed or misunderstood." As you may have noticed, these words are reminiscent of what you learned in Habit 3, helping you stimulate a collaborative mindset and communicate for understanding. And if you do miss or misunderstand something, know this, "A bad day for the ego is a good day for the soul"[45] as Robin Sharma, leadership expert and author likes to say.

Step 2: Insert your wisdom
(to signal competence)

In this step, think of yourself as a curator who's aggregating hidden and unorthodox insights, trends, or patterns related to the topic in question. Or a thought leader providing a unique perspective that sparks an alternative path for thinking. Keep it succinct, focused, and punchy to avoid losing their focus. Remember, less is more. Not only will this signal competence, but it will slowly increase your credibility stock as you subtly attempt to teach them something they didn't know before they spoke to you. However, refrain from being prescriptive or giving unsolicited advice until you've progressed the conversation and understood that person's language of service (as outlined in Habit 2). If somebody doesn't feel safe enough to admit that you've uncovered a blind spot, that's okay. As long as a collaborative and strategic conversation ensues, your Trusted Guide Message is working its magic.

Step 3: Ask a Storyworthy Question
(to stimulate a consultative conversation)

As we outlined in Habit 2, a Storyworthy Question (a.k.a. an open-ended question) allows you to extract a story or provoke deep thought and stimulate silence, telling somebody a story of intention about you. Both outcomes are welcomed, with the latter being the holy grail.

Here are a few examples for you to chew on:

- "I noticed you nodded when I mentioned my first idea, could you tell me more about what stood out to you?"
- What was the moment you first realized this specific trend was a problem for the business?
- If you could pick just one industry trend right now that's directly impacting the KPIs you care about, which one would you choose and why?

Something to take note of: In our first example, notice how it shows the importance of paying attention to what's not being said while you're speaking. This may feel difficult at first. However, as you move up the conscious competence ladder and strengthen your listening skills, your intuition and emotional intelligence will naturally grow louder. Ultimately, the key lies in asking a Storyworthy Question that helps you move the conversation forward.

I can't say this enough, but keep your Trusted Guide Message punchy and keep it brief. Verbal vomiting all over the person in question and delivering a Shakespearean monologue will do everything but elevate your presence and neutralize any perceived status imbalance. When practiced and implemented with intention, these three simple steps will increase the chances of your becoming the trusted guide in someone's business and life.

As a culture, we're sick of reactive behavior, tired of transactional conversations, and starved for human connection. You, my friend, are going to cut through the noise, stand out in a sea of sameness, and give people what they truly want: a trusted guide. Someone with a long-term outlook, a service-first mindset, and the competency to help others realize their desires, free from self-interest. Remember, business is a marathon, not a 100-meter sprint.

When using the practices inside this habit, your energy and aura will become magnetic, rather than reeking of desperation from having a death grip on your desires. Not only that, but your behavior, presence, and demeanor will become an example for those around you. Over time, you'll become a symbol for others and build a legacy you're proud of. And that is the final stop on our journey: transforming yourself into a symbol, earning relationship currency that can't be bought, and achieving limitless influence.

THE HIGHLIGHT REEL

1. Being a trusted guide is about living a lifestyle where one has a long-term outlook, operates with a service-mindset, and competently helps others realize their desires, without self-interest.

2. Embody the behavior you want others to exhibit and allow silent influence to help you create change without preaching or giving unsolicited advice. Stop telling and start showing.

3. When asked a question you don't know the answer to, own your truth, stay in your zone of genius, and become the expert in finding the expert. This will increase your credibility stock.

4. Create a level-playing field with another human being who has more experience or expertise by simply illuminating something they didn't know before they met you, sparking a strategic, collaborative, and consultative conversation.

BE A SYMBOL

"As a man, I'm flesh and blood, I can be ignored, I can be destroyed; but as a symbol . . . as a symbol I can be incorruptible, I can be everlasting."

—BRUCE WAYNE

On a lazy Sunday afternoon in 2005, my dad took my sister and me to the cinema to kill our boredom. Little did I know that the movie we'd watch, *Batman Begins*, would one day spark a thread of inspiration that would eventually lead me to write my first book. In Christopher Nolan's depiction of Bruce Wayne, there's a scene that's been burned into my memory ever since that first viewing. Bruce is sitting on his private jet with Alfred, his butler and confidant, after vanishing from Gotham City for several years, secretly preparing his mind, body, and spirit to fight injustice as a vigilante.

He says to Alfred, "People need dramatic examples to shake them out of apathy, and I can't do that as Bruce Wayne. As a man, I'm flesh and blood, I can be ignored, I can be destroyed; but as a symbol . . . as a symbol, I can be incorruptible, I can be everlasting."

111

In the world of business, our addiction to instant gratification is stealing our energy, joy, and long-term fulfillment. Your prospects, customers, partners, employees, team, and more need dramatic examples to shake them out of apathy. When you embody the five communication habits laid out in this book, your presence won't be ignored, and your reputation won't be destroyed. In a time where we're starved of human connection, your personal journey of becoming incorruptible will allow your example to be everlasting. The side effects are inspiring change that ripples across generations to come and leaving a legacy. This allows you to achieve limitless influence.

When I think of somebody who has achieved this in its purest form, I instantly think of Halim Demir.

NOT JUST A TAILOR, BUT A SYMBOL

If you've ever worked with me, hired me, or seen me speak, you'll know that I am obsessed with wearing a meticulously tailored suit with a clean and refined appearance that reflects my energy. Quintessentially British, right? Single button, double-breasted, corduroy fabric—I don't care; I love them all! And when it comes to finding a perfectly fitted suit that hits the spot, there's only one man on planet Earth that I trust: Halim, the owner of a suit tailor in London.

Let's take it back for a second.

Back in 2013, while a custom-fitted suit was out of reach for my bank balance, I still had a desire to walk into the office every single morning feeling confident and magnetic. The next best alternative was a custom-fitted shirt. However, when I began my search, I was horrified to learn about the investment required to help me realize my desires. Feeling deflated, I grudgingly walked into a run-of-the-mill suit store nearby and succumbed to their offer of buying five shirts for about £120 (or a little over $160). As I headed to the till and admitted defeat, a gentleman unknowingly handed me the keys to my kingdom: "Hello, Sir, would you like to have those shirts tailored?" Hold on, I could buy a shirt off the peg, have it tailored for a fraction of the cost, *and* still walk around the office thinking I'm the brown Bruce Wayne!? Say no more. I was all in.

Ten days later, I rushed to the suit store to try on my shirts, hoping they would fit like a glove. Instead, I received a set of shirts so tight that I looked like I belonged in a '90s boy band. Alteration after alteration, and I still didn't feel seen, heard, or understood. They struggled to get it "just right." And then I realized the disconnect. This run-of-the-mill suit store didn't have an in-house tailor. Instead, they outsourced their work to a boutique tailor who had the contract for all of their stores across London. So, I decided to cut out the middleman and go straight to the source!

One ice-bitingly cold Saturday evening, I grabbed my shirts, jumped in my car, and headed straight to the boutique tailor. Just a few minutes from the store, I couldn't find my bearings. Those few minutes turned into ten, which led to half an hour. I called the store in a huff and a puff, and a man with a calm, gentle, and warm voice picked up the phone with a smile (I could even hear it). "Halim here, how can I help you?" Within sixty seconds of me explaining the nearest landmarks around me, Halim got in his car and came to find me. Apparently, I was just around the corner (but hey, my weak navigation skills are beside the point).

As I walked into his idyllic store filled with beautiful chinos, shirts, shoes, and more, I quickly realized that Halim wasn't an employee working late on a Saturday night; he was the owner. From offering me traditional Turkish tea, to welcoming me into his store as if it were his home, it was crystal clear that this man knew he wasn't in the tailoring business; he was in the people business.

See, Halim first stumbled upon his genius for tailoring when he was just twelve years old back in his hometown in Turkey. Then, in the late '90s, he decided to immigrate to London, where he kickstarted his tailoring career, working on the famous Savile Row for a decade. In 2013, he founded his first flagship store in central London, the very one I had just walked into. Today, celebrities, entrepreneurs, and professionals across London visit Halim's shops to receive their desires in the form of fashion.

As you know, I have a soft spot for the immigrant hustle and can only imagine what risks Halim had to take, from a kid starting out in Turkey, to pursuing his passion in the UK, and eventually growing his own business from scratch. The dedication to his craft, his energy, and the number of years he's been in business tells me one thing. His story has been a personal development journey in disguise, requiring constant evolution and shifts in his internal story (remember Habit 1?) to ensure he's capable of receiving and sustaining his authentic desires: a thriving family-run business.

As I was browsing and nosing around his store, Halim asked me to try on one of the shirts I had brought with me. As he measured me up, he started the conversation by being interested in me, without focusing on trying to be interesting. His chosen vehicle? Conscious questions. As he asked me a series of Storyworthy Questions (as you learned in Habit 2), he effortlessly extracted a plethora of stories and information from me like a secret agent working for the government. And I'll tell you what: I loved every minute of it. I felt seen and taken care of, and I believed he deeply cared. Not because he told me, but because he showed me. By listening to my every word, learning exactly how I wanted to feel the moment I put those shirts on, and replaying my vision back to me, Halim made me feel like I truly mattered in his presence (just as we dug into in Habit 3). Halim embodied true charisma.

As he continued his discovery process into me and my needs, he subtly injected a short social proof story (which you learned how to craft in Habit 4) about other men "just like me" who had a similar pain (looking like a '90s boy band member) and desired transformation (feeling like their equivalent of the brown Bruce Wayne). As we walked to the till, he began calculating the cost of tailoring all five of my shirts. I leaned in with shifty eye contact and sheepishly whispered, "So, erm, what's the cost?"

Tap, tap, tap.

As he bashed away at his calculator, he slowly looked up at me, looked back down, and started slashing the price left, right, and center. After a brief pause, he turned the calculator toward me with a smile and said, "How about this?" In that moment, Halim instantly became my trusted guide (just like you learned how to become in Habit 5). He didn't focus on making a quick buck; instead, he focused on embracing a long-term outlook and helped me realize my desires without self-interest. Relationship currency had been earned alongside a customer for life.

From the moment I met Halim, he showed a capacity for connecting with me on a deeper level, integrity that told me a story about his character, and elite competence every step of the way. As you may remember, connection, character, and competence are the Three C's required for trust to be apparent in any business relationship.

Over ten years later, I still go to Halim's store. Not only do they still slash their prices at the till for me, but they do it with a smile. Whether it's a fresh new suit for a speaking gig or a perfectly tailored outfit for my wedding, Halim's been with me every step of the way. His team are the only people I deeply trust with this aspect of my life.

Over the years, I've subtly observed Halim and how he's become a symbol for others. Naturally, as his business grew, he didn't always have the opportunity to personally measure up every single customer's shirts, suits, and more. The first time I came to this realization was when one of his colleagues offered to serve me because Halim was away on a business trip. I was nervous. I felt the anxiety of someone getting a haircut from a brand-new hairdresser after years of going to the same person they loved.

However, to my surprise, Halim's value system, love for human connection, and care had diffused across his entire company. And it wasn't by accident. Whether it's remembering my children's ages, asking how my wife is doing, offering me traditional Turkish tea, or asking me conscious questions that go beneath the surface, Halim's vision and values are deeply embedded across his entire team. They aren't playing the game of business like it's a 100-meter sprint. Every single person inside the company is playing the game like it's a lifelong marathon. This, my friends, is how you become a symbol and achieve limitless influence.

BEING A SYMBOL

What does this mean for you? If you're somebody whose job is to transform prospects into paying customers or grow an existing customer portfolio, being a symbol means detaching from the "sale" and guiding someone from pain to glory while suspending your self-interest, so your prospect or customer can become the hero of their own story.

If you're somebody who leads people in an organization, being a symbol can mean making others feel significant in your presence.

And it can mean inspiring change, first within yourself, and then in the people you serve, by guiding others by example and embodying the change you wish to see.

If you're somebody who runs a business or has an entrepreneurial flare and is looking to step out on your own, being a symbol can mean pursuing a desire and vision that amplifies your genius, building an inspiring workplace culture and telling magnetic stories that motivate action, both internally and externally.

Every single one of these cases requires you to embody the five communication habits in this book so you can increase your influence, build trusted relationships and receive your definition of success.

YOU HAVE LIMITLESS INFLUENCE

As I look back at the different chapters of my own story, one thing is as clear as day. I am an imperfect human being, just like you. I've chased desires driven by ego and rooted in instant gratification. I've told myself stories that unknowingly caused self-sabotage, dimmed my light and led me to play small. I've asked unconscious questions and neglected deep listening. I've made myself look significant at the expense of somebody else feeling significant. I've told stories that dampened my influence. And I've behaved in ways that were at odds with the lifestyle of a trusted guide. I mean, haven't we all?

Rather than hold previous versions of myself hostage for their mistakes, I now give those versions grace and acknowledge that they did the best they could with the level of awareness they had at the time. As a fellow student of life, I invite you to do the same, my friend.

I also invite you to look back, reflect on your own journey and connect the dots. Why? Because you'll realize that every villain encountered, trusted guide met, and lesson learned was secretly serving your future self. Once again, everything happens for us, not to us. As you move forward with your perfectly imperfect journey and strive to become a symbol for others, remember this: earning relationship currency is your golden ticket for limitless influence and business success.

ENDNOTES

1   Action Learning Center, 2024. "Preparing the Ground for Learning." Accessed May 15, 2025. https://www.actionlearningcentre.com/preparing-the-ground-for-learning/.

2   Revolution Learning and Development Ltd. "The Conscious Competence Learning Model—Revolution Learning and Development Ltd," n.d. https://www.revolutionlearning.co.uk/article/conscious-competence-learning-model/.

3   Behar, H. (2009). *It's Not About the Coffee: Lessons on Putting People First from a Life at Starbucks*. Penguin Publishing Group.

4   Magazine, Ceo. "Scrub Daddy: The Story Behind Shark Tank US's Biggest Success." *The CEO Magazine*, April 17, 2020. https://www.theceomagazine.com/business/innovation-technology/scrub-daddy-the-story-behind-shark-tank-uss-biggest-success/.

5   Shark Tank Global. "A Bidding War Breaks Out During Scrub Daddy's Pitch | Shark Tank US | Shark Tank Global," February 25, 2022. https://www.youtube.com/watch?v=ae5MssJ8en4.

6   "How I Made Over $220M in Sales as the Daddy of the Scrub Daddy," February 2, 2024. https://fortune.com/videos/watch/how-i-made-over-%24220m-in-sales-as-the-daddy-of-the-scrub-daddy/ac1f281f-1c40-4969-99ca-1cac131f540b.

7   Kmrshubham. "How Much Did Lori Make From Scrub Daddy? The Numbers Will Surprise You." *Startup Booted* (blog), March 14, 2025. https://www.startupbooted.com/how-much-did-lori-make-from-scrub-daddy.

8   Farez, Kevin Sanchez. "Scrub Daddy's Famous Sponge Was Rejected by a Fortune 500 Company and Forgotten in a Box for Years. It's Now a $220 Million Empire." Fortune, February 2, 2024. https://fortune.com/2024/02/02/scrub-daddy-founder-interview-shark-tank-success-story/.

9   Stephan Spencer, host, *Get Yourself Organized*, episode 140, "Reining in Your Reactivity with Kabbalah," accessed July 28, 2025, https://www.getyourselfoptimized.com/reining-in-your-reactivity-with-kabbalah-david-ghiyam/.

10 Kircher, Madison Malone. "The Meaning of Influence, Written in the Stars." *Times Insider*. March 30, 2024. https://www.nytimes.com/2024/03/09/insider/influence-word-origin.html.

11 "Influence Noun—Definition, Pictures, Pronunciation and Usage Notes | Oxford Advanced Learner's Dictionary at OxfordLearnersDictionaries.com," n.d. https://www.oxfordlearnersdictionaries.com/definition/english/influence.

12 "Global Report," 2024. https://www.edelman.com/sites/g/files/aatuss191/files/2024-02/2024%20Edelman%20Trust%20Barometer%20Global%20Report_FINAL.pdf.

13 Yale School of Management. "Zoe Chance," n.d. https://som.yale.edu/faculty-research/faculty-directory/zoe-chance.

14   Chance, Zoe. *Influence Is Your Superpower: How to Get What You Want Without Compromising Who You Are.* Penguin Random House, 2023.

15   Nesterak, Evan. "Good Habits, Bad Habits: A Conversation With Wendy Wood—Behavioral Scientist." Behavioral Scientist, December 11, 2022. https://behavioralscientist.org/good-habits-bad-habits-a-conversation-with-wendy-wood/.

16   *Avoid labeling your child | Extension | University of Nevada, Reno.* (n.d.). Extension | University of Nevada, Reno. https://extension.unr.edu/publication.aspx?PubID=3011.

17   The Decision Lab. "Active Listening—the Decision Lab," n.d. https://thedecisionlab.com/reference-guide/psychology/active-listening.

18   Fisic, Jelena. "How to Engage in Deep Listening in the Workplace." *Pumble Blog* (blog), December 1, 2022. https://pumble.com/blog/deep-listening/.

19   "When Sadhana Becomes Successful," February 13, 2024. https://isha.sadhguru.org/en/wisdom/article/when-sadhana-becomes-successful.

20   *The what & why of sadhana.* April 25, 2023. https://isha.sadhguru.org/en/wisdom/article/the-what-why-of-sadhana

21   Sutton, Jeremy, Ph.D. "What Is Bandura's Social Learning Theory? 3 Examples." *Positive Psychology* (blog), May 17, 2021. Accessed March 19, 2025. https://positivepsychology.com/social-learning-theory-bandura/#what-is-banduras-social-learning-theory.

22   Carnegie, Dale. "How To Be More Interesting." Accessed April 9, 2025. https://www.dalecarnegie.com/en/dalecarnegieprinciples/how-to-be-interesting-person.

23   "Trailer for Chris Voss–Teaches the Art of Negotiation." Accessed April 9, 2025. https://www.masterclass.com/classes/chris-voss-teaches-the-art-of-negotiation/chapters/mirroring.

24   Staff, Loom. "Sawubona!—Loom International."
      Loom International, August 14, 2020. https://www.
      loominternational.org/sawubona/.

25   Gaunt, Derek. "Communication Skills: Hang a Label™
      on It." *Negotiation Mastery* (blog), November 17, 2023.
      Accessed March 19, 2025. https://www.blackswanltd.com/
      newsletter/hang-a-label-on-it?utm_campaign=Chris%20
      LinkedIn&utm_content=291106724&utm_medium=social&
      utm_source=linkedin&hss_channel=lis-i6P2SEqsO1.

26   "Charisma," March 19, 2025. https://dictionary.cambridge.
      org/us/dictionary/english/charisma.

27   Arabi, J. (2021, November 26). *Is a Sigh Just a Sigh?* https://
      governmentscienceandengineering.blog.gov.uk/2021/11/26/
      is-a-sigh-just-a-sigh/.

28   Motivational Speaker for Teachers—Josh Shipp. "Your
      Imperfections Make You Influential—Josh Shipp,"
      November 28, 2018. https://www.youtube.com/
      watch?v=cBiaCai6WDg.

29   "4 Consumer Insights About Online Reviews That Are
      Standing the Test of Time," n.d. https://business.trustpilot.
      com/blog/build-trusted-brand/4-things-every-business-owner-
      should-know-about-the-state-of-reviews.

30   DiSalvo, David. "Study: Receiving a Compliment Has Same
      Positive Effect as Receiving Cash." Forbes, November 9,
      2012. https://www.forbes.com/sites/daviddisalvo/2012/11/09/
      study-receiving-a-compliment-has-same-positive-effect-as-
      receiving-cash/.

31   Littlefield, Christopher. "Do Compliments Make You
      Cringe? Here's Why." *Harvard Business Review*, April 9,
      2021. https://hbr.org/2021/04/do-compliments-make-you-
      cringe-heres-why.

32 Messinger, Dr. (2008). Smiling. In *Encyclopedia of Infant and Early Childhood Development* (pp. 186–198). Elsevier Inc.

33 Cantor, Carla. "Are Your New Year's Resolutions Fading? Try a Different Approach." *Columbia News.* January 20, 2020. https://news.columbia.edu/news/resolutions-new-year-change-behavior-values.

34 Hansaj, Ekalavya. "Council Post: How Neuro-Linguistic Programming Can Help Your Advertising Business." Forbes, July 21, 2020. https://www.forbes.com/councils/forbesbusinesscouncil/2020/07/21/how-neuro-linguistic-programming-can-help-your-advertising-business/.

35 Christian, Kwame. "The Secret to Influence: Ask the Magic Question." Forbes, June 13, 2022. https://www.forbes.com/sites/kwamechristian/2022/06/13/the-secret-to-influence-ask-the-magic-question/.

36 Cialdini, Robert B. 2021. *Influence, New and Expanded: The Psychology of Persuasion.* Harper Business.

37 Clinic, Cleveland. "Brainwork: The Power of Neuroplasticity." Cleveland Clinic, September 9, 2024. https://health.clevelandclinic.org/neuroplasticity.

38 Asmus, Mary Jo. "The Neuroscience of Asking Insightful Questions." Government Executive, April 12, 2021. https://www.govexec.com/management/2017/04/neuroscience-asking-insightful-questions/137274/.

39 Zak, Paul J. "Why Your Brain Loves Good Storytelling." *Harvard Business Review.* Harvard Business Publishing, October 28, 2014. Accessed March 19, 2025. https://hbr.org/2014/10/why-your-brain-loves-good-storytelling.

40 "Albert Bandura, *Social Learning Theory* (Prentice-Hall, 1977).

41   Wim Hof Method. "Breathing Exercises." *Wim Hof Method*,
      n.d. https://www.wimhofmethod.com/breathing-exercises.

42   Zhao, Xin, Yi-Chun Yang, Gexin Han, and Qiao Zhang.
      "The Impact of Positive Verbal Rewards on Organizational
      Citizenship Behavior—The Mediating Role of Psychological
      Ownership and Affective Commitment." *Frontiers in
      Psychology* 13 (April 28, 2022). https://doi.org/10.3389/
      fpsyg.2022.864078.

43   Harvard Health. "Understanding the Stress Response," April
      3, 2024. https://www.health.harvard.edu/staying-healthy/
      understanding-the-stress-response.

44   You Exec. "Why Is Three Considered the Smallest
      Number of Elements Required," n.d. https://youexec.com/
      questions/why-is-three-considered-the-smallest-number-of-
      elements#:~:text=Three%20is%20considered%20the%20
      smallest,rule%2C%20thus%20creating%20a%20pattern.

45   Sharma, R. (2018). *The 5 AM Club: Own Your Morning.
      Elevate Your Life.* Harper Thorsons.

ABOUT THE AUTHOR

Ravi Rajani is an international keynote speaker, communication expert, and LinkedIn Learning instructor, with over sixty-five thousand professionals having taken his courses on Conscious and Charismatic Communication. Recognized globally as one of the top thought leaders in communication, Ravi has partnered with mission-driven leaders, teams, and organizations such as T-Mobile, Oracle NetSuite, and Sherwin-Williams to help them become effective communicators who build meaningful relationships that amplify revenue and foster a culture of trust.

Off stage and off camera, Ravi lives just outside London, United Kingdom, with his wife, son, daughter, and their furry little West Highland terrier. He loves the movie *Limitless*, a great stand-up comedian, and a sharp, quintessentially British suit.

To invite Ravi to speak to your organization about the five communication habits for building trust and cultivating business relationships that drive growth, or to inquire about additional services, please visit theravirajani.com.

theravirajani.com

in /theravirajani

@theravirajani

@theravirajani

@theravirajani

@theravirajani